THE KID-DOM OF GOD

Emmy
Abundant
Blessings!
Nac
Reeves

THE
KID-DOM
OF GOD

Helping Children Grow in Christian Faith

Roman Catholic Edition

Nancy Reeves and Linnea Good

Editor: Michael Schwartzentruber
Cover and Interior: Cyrus Gandevia
Proofreader: Dianne Greenslade
Cover image: © Zurijeta/Shutterstock

GOLD

BNC CERTIFIED | BIBLIOGRAPHIC DATA 2014-15

WoodLake is an imprint of Wood Lake Publishing, Inc. Wood Lake Publishing acknowledges the financial support of the Government of Canada through the Canada Book Fund (CBF) for its publishing activities. Wood Lake Publishing also acknowledges the financial support of the Province of British Columbia through the Book Publishing Tax Credit.

At Wood Lake Publishing, we practise what we publish, being guided by a concern for fairness, justice, and equal opportunity in all of our relationships with employees and customers. Wood Lake Publishing is committed to caring for the environment and all creation. Wood Lake Publishing recycles, reuses, and encourages readers to do the same. Resources are printed on 100% post-consumer recycled paper and more environmentally friendly groundwood papers (newsprint), whenever possible. A percentage of all profit is donated to charitable organizations.

Library and Archives Canada Cataloguing in Publication

Reeves, Nancy Christine, 1952-, author
        The kid-dom of God : helping children grow in Christian faith / Nancy Reeves and Linnea Good. -- Roman Catholic edition.

Issued in print and electronic formats.
ISBN 978-1-77064-791-6 (pbk.).--ISBN 978-1-77064-798-5 (html)

        1. Catholic children--Religious life. I. Good, Linnea, author II. Title.

BX2347.8.C5R44 2015   282.083   C2014-908305-X
                                               C2014-908306-8

Published by Woodlake
An imprint of Wood Lake Publishing Inc.
485 Beaver Lake Road, Kelowna, BC, Canada, V4V 1S5
www.woodlakebooks.com
250.766.2778

Printing 10 9 8 7 6 5 4 3 2 1
Printed in Canada

DEDICATIONS

From Nancy
To Bob, who has been and continues to be a
wonderfully supportive co-parent,
and to Christina who continues to teach us much
about being parents: *Gratias vobis ago.*

From Linnea
To Patrick, Nicole, and Isaac.
It would've been enough, and this is true. But still my
life burst open when it gave me you.

TABLE OF CONTENTS

ACKNOWLEDGEMENTS

A big thank you to Bernadette Gasslein, liturgist and editor of *Celebrate!* magazine, who approached us with the idea of a regular column on nurturing children's spirituality. Writing the column was a joyful, growing experience for us. Thanks to Mike Schwartzentruber for encouraging us to adapt the column to book format, and for the skillful and sensitive editing he brought to the project

CHAPTER 1

NURTURING SPIRITUALITY

You are a part of everything –
the seas, the ground and the sky
This is the love that planted the earth,
the Spirit's reason why.

"Part of Everything" by Linnea Good, from her CD *Sunday Sessions*

A worried grandmother drew Nancy aside at a workshop: "My daughter and her husband no longer attend Mass. How will my grandchildren come to know God?"

Nancy's response was not what the woman expected: "Children already experience God even before anyone talks to them about spiritual things," she said. "Trust that the Holy Spirit is active in the lives of your grandchildren, and ask God in prayer what part you are to play in their spiritual formation."

God is in loving relationship with us before birth. Tenderly, the prophet Jeremiah speaks God's words to us: "Before I formed you in the womb I knew you, and before you were born I consecrated you" (1:5). The psalmist prays, "For it was you who formed my inward parts; you knit me together in my mother's womb" (Psalm 139:3).

The grandmother contacted Nancy three weeks later and said, "I took my concern to prayer and sensed God saying, 'Be Christ to them.' So I have let go of my worry and am being loving and compassionate instead. I've stopped nagging my daughter to take them to church. Already my relationship with her and her husband is warmer and more relaxed. With the children, I'm talking about how God is in my life and they are very receptive. I realize that, before, I was trying to work *for* God rather than *with* God."

It's always helpful and good to remember that whatever we do to deepen or develop faith in ourselves or with those we love, we do in partnership with the Holy Spirit. Ralph Mattson and Thom Black have a wonderful analogy in their book

Discovering Your Child's Design. They suggest that we become "gardeners" who *nurture* our children's spirituality rather than "architects" who attempt to design and build it. As gardeners, we want to help children value their spiritual nature so that it can become deeper and sustain them through life. We do this by acknowledging, affirming, and providing words for the child-God relationship that is already developing within them.

Storytelling is one of the best ways to do this. When we hear a story, we automatically imagine ourselves in the plot and are often therefore more receptive to the meaning God wishes us to take from the tale. We need to share the stories of our heritage: the stories of Jesus' life, his parables, other Bible accounts and stories of God working in people of faith through the ages.

Each of these stories is important in itself. But the sacred stories' best purpose lies in showing us how each person's life is a "faith story," too.

Children need to become comfortable telling their *own* story, but how does this happen? We believe that it is as simple, and as difficult, as listening to children and sharing with them our *own* stories of God in our lives. The following is taken from the "Notes for Adults" section in *Adventures of the God Detectives*.

Sharing our spiritual experiences with children
Talking to children about experiences of God we had when we ourselves were children, or even after we became adults, may help them in many ways. They may begin to realize, for example, that divine/human interaction is normal and common. They may begin to understand that God relates to us in many different ways. Talking to children about our spiritual experiences can also give them spiritual language. And sharing important experiences of any kind may develop stronger bonds between the adults and children involved.

Telling children about our spiritual experiences can also be *unhelpful*. Children may judge our experiences as more important than their own. Or they may stop their sharing and politely switch from speaking to listening. Here are some tips for sharing our own faith stories or "God touches," intended to affirm and support the child's experiences.

HELPING CHILDREN

1. Prior to talking with a child, spend some time remembering your own childhood spiritual experiences. How were your heart and mind stirred by the divine? Write those experiences down or talk to another adult first. Many adults rarely – if ever – speak about their spiritual experiences. The first few times may feel awkward. If you can't remember any spiritual experiences, bring to prayer your desire to hear and see how God has been present in your life. Doing this may help memories to surface.

2. Sharing our experiences tends to take the conversational "ball" away from the child. After you tell your story, give the ball back, by saying something like, "So that's what happened when I was six. Can you tell me more about what happened to you?" If you just fall silent after telling your story, the child may not realize it is now their turn to talk.

3. Keep your sharing short, or kids may lose interest or be overloaded with information.

4. Never say, "The same thing happened to me." Your story will always have similarities and differences to the child's. Be more tentative: "I'll tell you a story about something that happened to me, which may be a bit like your experience." Let the child make his or her own connections.

5. Sharing our experiences is more helpful when those experiences are on a similar "level" to the child's story. If the child speaks of feeling "one with the whole world" and you have never had this feeling, it is enough to listen respectfully instead of sharing a different type of spiritual experience of your own. Similarly, children may feel diminished if you respond to their small divine "touches" with a mind-blowing dream of angels taking you to the throne of God.

Like so many other things in life, speaking about our spiritual experiences can feel unfamiliar and intimidating – like something best left to the experts. But perhaps it is far less complicated than we think. We can share with children the things that leave us awestruck, that make us wonder, that are radiant coincidences; dreams that leave us feeling at peace, heartaches we are still trying to understand… When we are open to the mystery of our own faith, we need not fear that we have to come up with all the answers. Join the children in the questions; God is there.

Song and Resource References

"Leaning on the Everlasting Arms," Anthony Showalter, from Linnea Good's CD *Swimmin' Like a Bird.*

CHAPTER 2

DISCERNMENT

Five-year-old Nancy was playing in the basement of her home, her father working nearby with power tools, when suddenly the electricity failed, plunging the house into darkness. Out of the black, Nancy heard her father: "Nancy, come over here." The fear in his voice reverberated through the girl; with her whole being she wanted to obey. She took a few halting steps, but then walked no further. She had "heard" another voice.

"Stop there," said the inner voice, with a gentle firmness that held her in place. "I halted and didn't move again – even when my father's demands grew in angry urgency. The quiet voice stayed with me until the lights came on a short time later." When Nancy's father looked at the ground in front of her in the spreading light, his expression of anger changed to one of horror. "I cannot remember what he saw," she says, "but I can remember what he said: 'Oh, my God, if you had taken one step forward you would have been severely injured! Why didn't you come when I called?' As he picked me up and held me against his shoulder, I don't know if he heard my muffled response: 'God told me not to move.'"

A special kind of decision making

Spiritual discernment is the art of listening for the guidance of the Holy. It is an important virtue because we believe that every decision, large and small, "goes better with God." God has given us gifts of reason and intuition and, when we use those faculties, we are using God's gifts of discernment. However, spiritual discernment not only uses our God-given skills, it invites God's active involvement in the decision-making process. We open ourselves to God's guidance, love, and direction as we bring our question into prayerful living. Because of this, the fruits of spiritual discernment are different and greater than simple discernment:

• Spiritual discernment helps us grow in faith and our relationship with God. When we trust that God is offering guidance, in the way and pace that we most need it, we are likely to develop more patience with ourselves and with God about the "outcome."

• Because we are prayerfully open to God's guidance through the everyday events of our lives, we may be more open to the people around us – any one of whom might be the bearer of God's "word" when we need to hear it.

• There may be better solutions to a question or problem than the ones we are most immediately aware of. God can help us see these other solutions when we ask for help.

• In fact, at times we may be considering the wrong question or problem. We may be stuck in a particular way of thinking, a well-worn rut of logic, asking the same people for advice on a predictable question. When we pray to God to open us to new possibilities, we are making a courageous invitation to bring about real change in our lives.

• God does not simply send us off in a direction, but will often show us how to follow that guidance, supporting us in grace as we make that journey. Often people will speak in retrospect about a particularly difficult time of their life when all they could do was pray and carry on. "I don't know where the strength came from," they will say. God's support is there for all of us to draw upon, even before we ask the question. When Frances asked the Holy Spirit for help with her difficult decisions, all she heard back were words from scripture: "Come to me, all you that are weary and are carrying heavy burdens, and I will give you rest" (Matthew 11:28). On the surface, this did not seem to be an answer to her question, yet she took the guidance. After a day off to relax, she found she had the clarity and strength to tackle her problems.

Children have a remarkable radar for the presence of the Spirit, and a willingness to listen for God's leading. Last year during the Lenten "Mission" at St. Gerard's in Calgary, the children were given some group divine guidance that proved very moving. As the evening program closed, the children returned to the sanctuary and, climbing the stairs to the chancel, sang a closing song of gratitude. Their singing was reverent, heartfelt, and joyous. When the applause ended, Linnea asked the children to return to their adults while everyone sang the closing hymn for the evening. Not one child moved; something within them said to stay. During the closing hymn, the children, some of them under three years old, did not budge from the chancel. They stood as a group, focused and resolved. It looked like there was something more for them to do. Nancy wondered if this were a "nudge" from God.

Earlier in the evening, the adults had blessed the children as they went off to their spiritual activities by forming an arch with their hands, under which the children marched, singing Linnea's song *And on This Path*. Following a hunch, Nancy invited the children to follow her now. The children caught on, quickly lined the aisles and, with big grins on their faces, waited as every adult in the room slowly walked under the arch of blessing they had created.

The adults moved slowly; many thanked the children. Some had tears in their eyes, some laughed and smiled. It took a long, long time before the last adult made their way out of the sanctuary. The blessing was shared by all.

HELPING CHILDREN

Have the awareness that God guides children in many ways. God may "speak" to your child through you; through other people; through dreams, scripture, favourite books, or nature, as well as through an inner feeling of rightness or peace, etc.

Be open with children about your own ways of receiving guidance from God. Speaking to our children about our own experiences will make discernment more understandable to them.

Some of the most exciting stories in scripture are about discernment. So read the stories to children, draw their attention to them during worship, and discuss them: "Today we heard about how God spoke to Joseph in a dream, to tell him to escape to Egypt with Mary and baby Jesus. God sometimes speaks to us in dreams. Have you ever had a dream where it felt like God was trying to tell you something?"

Often, when adults think of spiritual discernment, they focus on "methods," such as various prayer techniques. Although learning discernment methods is useful, we view discernment more as an *attitude* than a method. God may speak to us at any time, in any place. If we *do* use a method, we believe that the Spirit has called us to that particular way of discernment. We can practice the attitude of discernment and encourage our children to do so, too.

Song and Resource References

"How Then Shall I Live," Linnea Good, from her CD *Greatest of These.*

CHAPTER 3

DISCERNMENT - PART 2

"Hello, my name is Tyler. When my great-grandmother passed away, I was torn away inside. I had a box of all the stuff that reminded me of her. I would keep it open all the time. It made me feel better. When I felt I didn't need her in my life at that time, I would close the box.

"Once I had the box open around Christmas and my great-grandfather was sick. I was crying because he was going to die. I was thinking of him and all of a sudden the box closed. I thought it was just because the box had been touched earlier or something, but then I realized I didn't need her at the moment. I needed my great-grandfather and needed to be with him to help him on his last days. I have never told anyone this. Thank you."

This email came to us from a young boy. We have changed his name and some spelling, but all the words are his. Tyler wrote to tell us how God had guided him to see that he was focusing too much on the past and not being aware of a present need.

Did God close Tyler's box? Some would say "yes," others "no." We say, "It doesn't matter." The key is that God put an understanding in Tyler's heart and mind, which encouraged him to change his attitude and behaviour. God often guides us by "nudging" our attention toward something and giving us a message through that thing.

We believe that spiritual discernment – being open to divine guidance – is more of an attitude than a method. If we believe Jesus when he said he would send us his Spirit as advocate and guide, then we will look to see how the Spirit is working in our lives 24/7 to encourage us to make choices that are for the highest good. So let's explore some qualities and practices that we can foster in ourselves and in our children, so that we can more effectively hear and understand God's guidance.

Recently, Nancy had a conversation with some youth. One person told the group the following story.

"My church was trying to discern what to do with some money that had been given to us. Our pastor asked us all to pray and let him know if we heard a message from God. Later that day I *did* pray, but I kept hearing a new song that I really liked. I started to get mad at myself because I was trying to talk to God and I kept hearing that song. Then I started laughing, because I listened more closely to the words. They were about showing love for someone by inviting them into your life. I thought back at God, 'So should we start a program to invite more people into our church?' and I felt a warm feeling in my stomach. I told my pastor about the message. After about a month, he told the congregation that many people had had messages about holding a series of free talks about faith for the public. Our church would offer 'food' for their minds, hearts, and spirits. I helped out serving refreshments afterwards, so we fed their bodies too."

HELPING CHILDREN

In her research on spiritual discernment for her book *I'd Say Yes, God, If I Knew What You Wanted,* Nancy found a number of qualities and pre-requisites that help children and adults "hear" God's guidance more effectively.

1. ***Daily spiritual practice:*** Spiritual practices focus us more fully on God's presence in our lives, making it is easier to recognize guidance when it comes. Planned prayer time, such as grace before meals and bedtime devotions, is important. It also helps to encourage children to use spontaneous prayers of gratitude, sadness, openness, etc.

2. ***Self-awareness:*** Self-awareness helps us to discriminate between the voice of our ego (our small self), the "voices" of society, the opinions of others, and the "voices" of the Spirit. Understanding our strengths, gifts, and challenges is crucial to knowing what to ask for; for example, "God, please help me to be more loving to my baby brother when he takes my toys." We can help

children grow to self-awareness by giving them words for their personal characteristics and talking about our own.

3. **Right living:** If we neglect or harm ourselves, others, or our world, we may distort or misunderstand the messages we receive from God. This has sometimes caused faithful people to do unfaithful things, such as attempt to "force" the gospel on others, or to endanger themselves by remaining in abusive situations.

4. **Inclusive Receptivity:** Knowing that God may "speak" to us anywhere and at any time keeps us receptive, both to God and to the world.

5. **Patience:** True patience means living fully into the now, where God is, rather than just "enduring" the time until the anticipated event occurs.

6. **Trust:** Trust is an attitude in which we understand God as an active, loving force in our lives. Clare shared the following with her teen group:

"I don't think I have ever received a message from God."

In the discussion that ensued, Nancy suggested, "Many people don't get the message, 'Do this' from God. What they *do* get is the message, 'I love you.' This message can put us in a better frame of mind, with the result that we can often see more clearly the best path to take."

Clare responded, "Oh, yes, I get that message! Sometimes it feels like God is loving me through my friends, through scripture, or in nature. For sure, when I am feeling loved I make more loving decisions."

7. *Active participation:* Using our own unique gifts and talents allows us to partner with God in loving action.

8. *Gratitude:* Gratitude is being thankful for our relationship with God, for guidance already received, and for guidance that we know we will receive in the future.

All these qualities can enhance our ability to hear and understand the guidance of the Holy in our lives. Why not choose one of these qualities and, for a period of time, through prayer, invite God to bless you with that particular gift. You may just find yourself tuned in to the rich conversation God is wishing to have with you.

Song and Resource References

"There Is Your Heart," Linnea Good, from her CD *Greatest of These.*

CHAPTER 4

EGO

Sr. Mary Cabrini looked at me and exclaimed, "I didn't teach them that!"

We turned to face the 25 six- to eight-year-olds sitting in a circle around us. "Help, God!" I prayed silently. I had asked the group of children where the voices in our head – and in particular those voices that guide us in negative directions – come from. A young boy had just asserted that the negative voice within him was the devil.

I was giving a workshop at the Ursuline Sisters' spirituality centre in Louisville, Kentucky, reading stories from the book Linnea and I had written called *Adventures of the God Detectives*. The book is about a club made up of four friends aged seven to nine, searching for clues to the ways God speaks to people.

In the book, nine-year-old Fu-Han goes into the kitchen to get a glass of water. There he smells the delicious aroma of fresh-baked chocolate chip cookies. As he gazes at the cookies, he is "spoken to" by two voices. One voice tells him all the reasons why he should take a cookie: he is hungry, these are his *favourite* cookies, no one would know, and besides, his parents love him and would want him to have a treat... The other voice explains that taking a cookie without asking is actually stealing. After painful deliberation, Fu-Han turns away from the cookies, deciding that his need for honesty and for people's trust is of greater importance.

The students were wide-eyed. "Do you hear voices like that?" I asked. With a chorus of YESes, every hand went up, including Sr. Mary Cabrini's.

"What would you call those voices?"

A girl offered that the second voice was the voice of our conscience. All the children nodded. Sr. Mary Cabrini smiled. "And what about the first voice?" I asked.

"That's the voice of the Devil in us," said the boy. The children nodded knowingly. Sister Mary Cabrini and I were horrified.

I needed to think how I would respond. "No," I said finally. "That voice in your head is *not* the

Devil. It's what grownups call our ego or 'small self.' It isn't evil or bad; God wouldn't put something bad in us. The ego just isn't as wise as our conscience. Our ego is the part of us that only sees the little picture of a situation. When you just see the little picture, you can do things that suit you just fine, but that can hurt other people. Our conscience understands more; it sees the bigger picture. God sees the *biggest* picture of all and wants what is best for everyone."

So many of the stories that have captured the imagination of our culture seem to reinforce a childhood belief that the world is all-or-nothing; people are either 100% good or 100% evil. Sagas such as *Harry Potter*, *Narnia*, *Star Wars*, and *Lord of the Rings* seem to portray a struggle between forces that are either all good, or all bad. As children mature, they begin to realize that everyone is capable of doing both good *and* bad things, and that, when we do "bad" things, it is often out of ignorance or because of our woundedness.

Our ego is what we might think of as our "conscious self." A person who loves herself is emotionally healthy and is therefore more able to love God and other people. Children ideally develop a strong, healthy ego as they grow. Jesus spoke about this when he said that the necessary second half of the Great Commandment to love God is to love your neighbour "as you love yourself."

Unfortunately, the ego has received bad press. There has been a perception that we can only mature if we "destroy" or "transcend" our ego. Spirituality books sometimes refer to "ego" as our "false self." Not so! Certainly our ego can have unhealthy aspects, but it is still the core of who we are. Personal renovation involves partnering with God to refine our ego, strengthening its healthy parts.

It can be helpful to parents and leaders to know that children become egocentric – that is, very concerned with self – during developmental periods when much physical, mental, and emotional change is taking place. So four-year-olds and 14-year-olds may think of themselves first, while the nine-year-old may be much more concerned with others. Yet once these children feel their own needs have been met, they can be very compassionate towards others.

At the end of the session, Nancy asked the students in the religion class how they responded when a baby brother or sister did something they shouldn't do. A young girl had an answer: "You don't hurt them. You use firm love. Then, if they won't listen, you go and get a grownup."

"Great!" said Nancy. "That's just what to do if your ego tells you to do something you know is wrong. Use firm love."

HELPING CHILDREN

1. Share with children your own struggles with the two voices. "My boss was away sick today, so she wouldn't have known if I left work early. One voice told me I was tired and it would be good to go home. But I'm glad I listened to my conscience which said to stay. My boss trusted me and that's important to me."

2. Instead of blaming children for being selfish, invite them to "think like a team" or "show leadership in the family by..."

3. Tell children that if they *do* "hear" a voice or experience something that feels really scary or evil, to ask God to give them strength and to tell a grownup right away.

4. When children "confess" to doing something wrong, praise them for their awareness that they did wrong and for their honesty and willingness to tell you. Rather than dwelling on the negative, treat it as a challenge to solve. You might say something like, "Now you have a problem; you have done something wrong and need to find a way to make it right again. I can help you think of ways you might solve this problem and I have confidence that you can do what you need to do to fix it." Punishments encourage resentment, shame, and embarrassment, which can actually undermine the ego's growth. Reconciliation means encouraging the desire to act justly – especially through actions that right the wrong.

So often we worry: "What if I get it wrong?" Of course it is natural to want to be effective and caring parents, grandparents, teachers, and youth leaders, but our own wounded egos can get in the way and judge us negatively, causing us to pull away from talking with children about their spiritual lives. It is both scary and encouraging to know that the greatest part of our caregiving is not techniques and knowledge, but shown through who we really are. To embrace our own "ego" is part of the process of learning how to care compassionately for the little ones we love.

Song and Resource References

"Who Am I?" composer unknown, from Linnea Good's CD *Swimmin' Like a Bird*.

CHAPTER 5

DREAMS FROM GOD

On the way home from Mass, eight-year-old Jean told his dad about the Bible story he had heard. "Joseph was a boy and God sent him a dream, but his brothers got mad when they heard it and pushed him down a well."

"What do you think about that story?" his father replied.

"Well, the dreams God sends me aren't like that one."

His father was surprised: "I didn't know God has sent you dreams."

"You never asked," Jean stated.

"I'd like to hear about those dreams now," his dad said.

"The God ones don't happen a lot," mused Jean. "Sometimes Jesus is talking to me and sometimes I just feel a big Love. I can never remember what Jesus looked like when I wake up and I can't remember what he said, but I always feel really good and really loved. I think about them over and over. Regular dreams can be fun or exciting or scary, but the love isn't there, so I know which ones God sends."

"Thanks for telling me," his dad said, after some silence. "I've had some dreams that I thought God sent me, but I've never shared them with anyone. You're making me think it would be good to share our God dreams."

Jean grinned. "Yup – just don't push me down a well if you don't like it."

The scripture that Jean was referring to is Genesis 37:5–8.

Once Joseph had a dream, and when he told it to his brothers, they hated him even more. He said to them, "There we were, binding sheaves in the field. Suddenly my sheaf rose and stood upright; then your sheaves gathered around it, and bowed down to my sheaf." His brothers said to him, "Are you indeed to reign over us? Are you indeed to have dominion over us?" So they hated him even more because of his dreams and his words.

Many children have told us about dreams that they believe were sent to them by God.

Dr. Kate Adams, a senior lecturer at Bishop Grosseteste University College, in Lincoln, England, has been studying children's spiritual development for over a decade. Some of her research has focused on dreams that children believe to be of God or sent by God. In one study of 94 children, one third had not told anyone they had had a dream from God. Some children feared they would be ridiculed or had had experiences where a parent had told them the dream was imaginary. Others found their parents merely disinterested. Dr. Adams is deeply concerned about the negative impact this dismissal can have on children's spiritual lives. Her research indicates that many children experience at least one dream that is highly meaningful and can shape their thoughts and actions.

God may send us dreams to comfort or to guide, or just to let us know how loved we are. And dreams are just one way that God gives us messages. It is not helpful if adults make much of, or dismiss, dreams that children believe come from God.

If children don't share their God-dreams, it can be helpful to share your own: "I had a dream that was so full of love that I know it was God who sent it to me. I'm still feeling that love." Or, "I had a dream that I don't understand, but I know that God will send me more or find some other way to help me understand the message." On the other hand, if your child does share a dream, guard against the impulse to immediately jump in to share your own. The child may feel that yours is better and hold back from further sharing.

The following suggestions come from our book *Adventures of the God Detectives*, in the "Notes for Adults" section at the back of the book, and may help adults to encourage this aspect of the child's relationship with God.

HELPING CHILDREN

1. We need to respect the importance of each child's dream, neither telling them what it was about or dismissing the possibility that it might hold wisdom. If children are used to hearing and speaking about dreams, they will be more receptive to the divinely inspired ones.

2. Some adults show interest only if a child has a nightmare or other disturbing dream. Positive dreams are more likely to be ignored. We can show children that we value all dreams by routinely asking, "Did anyone dream last night?" at the breakfast table.

3. It may be tempting to try to analyze the child's dream, but it is probably not helpful. Let the meaning be between the child and God. If there is a meaning for the dreamer, it will continue to "work" in him or her until it surfaces. If a child asks you what you think it means, it might be better to redirect the question back to the child: "It's your dream; what does it say to you?" or "Why don't you ask God about that?"

4. Children may find it useful to keep a dream journal. If dreams are recorded through drawing or writing, the dreamer will become familiar over time with their own rhythms and symbols, and may become better able to discern the nudgings of God in their lives.

Dreams are just one of the many ways God reaches out to us. Some people do not remember their dreams, and our loving God will communicate with those folk in other ways. Sharing dreams, as with any other type of spiritual sharing, can be a faith nourishing activity.

Song and Resource References

"All through the Night," Welsh traditional, adapted and arranged by Linnea Good, from her CD *Momentary Saints*.

CHAPTER 6

IMAGINARY COMPANIONS

It may have happened like this...

"Benjamin, I have a task for you. I baked some extra bread this morning and I want you to take it out and sell it. We could certainly use the money."

"Where could I sell it? Everyone in the village bakes their own."

"Miriam told me that a prophet who heals is speaking up the mountain today. They expect thousands to come."

So Benjamin took five barley loaves and two fish up the mountain. He was astonished by the multitudes that were present and tried to attend to selling his wares, but he found himself drawn to the prophet and his stories about God and God's people. Slowly he made his way through the seated groups of people so he could get close enough to hear him. Settling on the grass, he was soon lost – or was it found – in the words of this Jesus.

Time went by and Benjamin became hungry. He heard Jesus ask his followers to find bread for all. One of the men with Jesus tersely answered, "Six months' wages wouldn't buy enough bread for each of them to get a little."

As Benjamin listened to the men, he heard a familiar voice inside him: "Ben, you could help. You have bread and fish." He thought back: "But they are for sale!" The voice "spoke" again. "

Benjamin thought another moment. Then he approached another of Jesus' followers. Wordlessly he offered all the food he carried. Andrew looked at him a moment in quiet surprise. Then he thanked him and turned to Jesus. "There is a boy here who has five barley loaves and two fish." And the next miracle began.

How wonderful it was that Benjamin offered the food he had. How improbable his gift. What prompted this child to give away all he had at that moment? What was that inner "voice" that guided him?

Seven-year-old Amy dreaded opening her lunch kit and finding her dessert, because she knew that Alexis would take it. Alexis always took desserts from others, and she threatened to exclude Amy from the circle of girls that hung out at recess if she told on her. Amy couldn't see that it was worth the conflict and the risk of losing friends to confront the bully.

That was when Mr. Sparkles arrived. Mr. Sparkles, a rainbow-coloured dolphin, first came into Amy's life as a comforter, when she had been hurt at preschool.

"You'll be okay, Amy," he said over and over again, his voice smooth as a rainbow. Now, Mr. Sparkles told Amy that a bully never stops bullying until somebody confronts them. "Ask the other girls to help you," he said. "You can do it together."

The next day, Amy and three girlfriends told Alexis that she could eat with them, but that she couldn't take their desserts anymore. To their surprise, Alexis agreed, and they slowly became friends.

God "speaks" to us in many ways. Many adults and children have experienced some type of inner guiding divine voice. This voice may come in one of many different forms and, for children, may actually take the form of what has often been called an "imaginary companion."

The appearance of an imaginary companion is a very common childhood experience. Current research suggests that 65 percent of children up to age seven may have imaginary companions. The imaginary companions can range from a pocket-sized purple elephant who makes the child laugh with silly jokes, to a 200-year-old man who comes into the child's life "whenever I have problems and want someone wise to talk to." The vast majority of imaginary companions function in the following ways. They

- love the child unconditionally
- identify and encourage the child's good qualities
- comfort the child when he or she is scared or in pain
- answer questions about life and death
- serve as a playmate and companion, particularly when the child is lonely.

Research shows that children with imaginary companions are very similar to children without them.

However, children with imaginary companions seem to have other benefits. They

- learn to see other people's point of view, and develop empathy at an earlier age
- are able to sit still and focus their attention for longer periods of time
- tend to watch significantly less television because their fantasy world is so entertaining.

All of these qualities greatly benefit the child's spiritual formation. Studies show that older children, adolescents and even some adults have imaginary companions. Because our society does not generally support imaginary companions after the preschool years, older children and adults rarely talk about their imaginary friends.

With such loving, life-giving functions being manifested, God is obviously present in these experiences. But how? Does the Holy Spirit become a rainbow-coloured dolphin for Amy? Is the 200-year-old man a guardian angel? Does God create the imaginary companion to meet the child's need? We can't know for certain. Yet we do know that imaginary companions can help our children develop spiritual gifts and self-esteem.

HELPING CHILDREN

1. Acknowledge the imaginary companion without trying to change it or to enter into direct contact with it, without the child's permission.

2. Show gratitude for all the ways God talks with us – including through imaginary friends.

3. Don't worry if the imaginary companion stays into adolescence. It is a healthy thing.

4. Don't worry if your child does *not* have an imaginary companion.

In a very few cases, imaginary companions are negative, blaming, or tell kids to do hurtful things. Adults can help by doing the same kinds of things they might do about "the monster under the bed." A parent might, for example,

- ask God to change the imaginary companion's heart to be more loving.
- ask God for another companion to deal with the first. Ask the child what kind of new companion they think God will send.
- ask the child to draw the negative companion, and then again with changes that will help it be happy and peaceful (for example, by changing its appearance or size).

The realm of the imagination is a liminal, sacred space – especially for the child. In it, all things are possible, new ideas are tested, the mystical is experienced. It is surely where the seeds of faith are sown. May we be respectful companions to children as they grow in God.

Song and Resource References

"Doubters," Linnea Good, from her CD *I Know You.*

CHAPTER 7

EXTROVERSION

Eighty-two-year-old Sr. Betty Janelle spoke about being five years old: "The first sentence that I remember hearing was 'Who winds her up in the morning?' This was asked by one of my older brother's friends, who was about 12 years old."

Sallie reminisced about being a toddler: "I have a large extended family, and the highlight of my week was seeing all of my cousins each Sunday. My folks have teased me all my life that my first friends outside the family were the baker and the milkman who came to the house. I was happy to talk with them!"

These women are describing themselves as spiritual extroverts. Extroverts often direct their attention and energy to the outside world of people and things. They are more prone to action than to contemplation. They make friends readily, adjust easily to social situations, and generally show warm interest in their surroundings. Introverts are more energized by time alone and need solitude to make sense of their experiences. Although we don't know the percentages, there are more extroverts than introverts in the world.

Sr. Betty and Sallie participated in Nancy's research on spiritual extroverts, for her book *Spirituality for Extroverts – And Tips for Those Who Love Them*. Many respondents initially had a common perception that introverted people are more spiritual than their extroverted counterparts. They believed their faith was "shallow" because they did not gravitate to quieter, more inwardly-directed spiritual practices. As author Fr. Richard Rohr says, "This cannot be true!"

Research shows that a preference for extroversion or introversion is partially "hard-wired" within us. Those acting in an extroverted way will have more activity in the back of their brains, while introverts will have more activity in the frontal lobes.

What was Jesus?

As far as we can tell, Jesus demonstrated both extrovert and introvert qualities. While taking a lot of "alone time" with God, he also gained and received energy by talking with and responding to others. Likewise, many of Nancy's research participants said that as they matured spiritually, their extroversion ebbed and flowed to meet the specific needs of the situation. We call this ability to move back and forth "omniversion": omni meaning "encompassing all."

The Eucharist is a wonderful training ground for omniverts, as the flow of the liturgy has times of both inwardly- and outwardly-directed devotion. Some parts of worship, such as quiet prayers, encourage a more inward focus. The Sign of the Peace, on the other hand, is not fully "lived" unless done in an extroverted manner, truly engaging with our brothers and sisters. Other parts of worship can be done in *either* an extroverted or introverted way. For example, during the hymns, some turn inward, feeling the music resonate deep in their hearts, while others are very aware of feeling the energy of the other singers as their voices mingle to praise and give thanks to God.

Truly going with this flow encourages us to use all parts of our brain and spirit, so that we are more able to love God with our whole being.

Extroverted spiritual practice

Prior to becoming omniverts, however, we first need to understand and honour our more familiar inclination. Danny, an extroverted teen, complained, "Every time Fr. Anthony says, 'Let us pray,' everyone closes their eyes and bows their heads. But I want to turn up my face and look at Jesus on the cross above the altar. I like to send my love spiralling out to God. But it's like we've all got to quiet down and be alone with God. You know when I feel most 'connected' spiritually? Singing! I feel everybody's energy – the Body of Christ. And I feel God singing with us. It's awesome."

Extroverts experience the God-in-relation-with-all, and may take great comfort in practices such as praying with others, cultivating spiritual friendships, and movement prayer, such as opening to God's presence while walking in the woods, or in spiritual dancing.

HELPING CHILDREN

1. Let children know that spiritual practices can be done in extroverted and introverted ways.

2. Actively affirm the lived-out faith of your extroverted children – such as supporting Danny if he wants to turn up his face in prayer – while being sensitive to those who pray in a more introverted way.

3. Incorporate both extroverted and introverted spiritual practices into your family rituals. Linnea chooses between the two at the dinner table with her husband, David, and their three children, depending on the way the family seems to be feeling.

   "Sometimes it is right to simply bow our heads (I love to do it in the restaurant!)," she says. "There it is more of an introverted devotion. However, on other nights, I often begin by saying, 'Take a look around this table and see the faces of people you love. Look at your plate and see that food has been prepared for you. Let's give God thanks for all our incredible blessings!'"

4. You might encourage "omniversion" by doing the following spiritual exercise either in a group of adults or with older children.

Sing a chant such as Linnea's *I Rejoiced!* (based on Psalm 122). The first few times, sing in the manner that seems most familiar. Then talk about your experience. Is it more extroverted or introverted? When you can all sing it easily, invite each person to shift to the other inclination. Extroverts would turn their attention inward, perhaps letting the song resonate deep in their core, while introverts would turn outward, perhaps being more aware of the other singers praising God.

Initially, this can be somewhat tricky, since it doesn't seem natural. The most effective way to make the shift is to have the desire to do so, and to ask for God's help. Don't just wrench your usual energy in the opposite direction. Extrovert energy turned inward can feel too constricted, resulting in jitteriness and boredom; introvert energy forced outward can feel too vulnerable and exposed. Even if one or more of you is not able to make the shift in that first practice, hopefully you will gain more respect for the ways of others. You might also take the time to discuss how other favourite spiritual practices could be experienced in both introverted and extroverted ways.

As we continue to assist children to "round out" their spiritual practices, our goal is to help them identify their own best ways of meeting God. Thus, we may all bring more of our own true selves to the loving relationship God so desires.

Song and Resource References

"I Am Amazing" – words: source unknown, music: Linnea Good – from Linnea Good's CD *Swimmin' Like a Bird.*

CHAPTER 8

LOVE!

In the beginning was the Word. And the Word was with God and the Word was God.

John 1:1

In J.R.R. Tolkien's *Lord of the Rings*, there is a species of creatures called the "Ents" – great tree-like beings who help Frodo and his companions fight the forces of evil. The Ents are a ponderous, un-warlike bunch, whose conversations could last seemingly forever because the size of each word is equal to the importance of the thing being described. Small, un-important Ent issues live as short syllables, while a word like "water" could take months to utter. I think of the Ents whenever I consider how ridiculously short the word "love" is.

What is love?

Children and adults use the word a lot. We hear it frequently. "Oh, I'd love to have that cellphone," "I love my little pony," "I love what you've done with your hair!" The term "love" is often used to mean "like."

True love is a very different experience. Phrases such as, "an intense feeling of tender affection and compassion," "a passionate feeling of desire," "devotion to another," "to adore and find irresistible," speak of a variety of experiences, each profound in its own way. Christian guides throughout the ages have spoken of how essential true love is to spiritual growth. Indeed: love is the hallmark of the Christian life.

We read in 1 John that "God is love." Spiritual growth is about knowing deeply that God loves each one of us. The 17th-century Puritan preacher Thomas Watson wrote, "Read the Scriptures, not only as a history, but as a love-letter sent to you from God."

It is impossible to love if we do not feel loved ourselves. Fr. John Main speaks of the importance of allowing ourselves to experience love. "To know ourselves loved is to have the depths of our own capacity to love opened up."

"God's love has been poured into our hearts through the Holy Spirit that has been given to us"

(Romans 5:5). This love that helps us heal and grow is a transfiguring love. It literally changes the way people see us and the way we see ourselves. There is an example of this in Matthew 17:1–7. Jesus and a few of his followers ascend a mountain, where he is transfigured and begins to glow. When we deeply give ourselves in love, we *do* glow. Phrases such as "walking on air," "the radiant bride," speak to the experience of transfiguration. Many people have spoken of a "glow" that they experience at times when they are deep in prayer. In this type of love, we lose ourselves in communion with God. The "glow" is a quickening, a new aliveness, the presence of the Holy Spirit within us. We put our whole body into living the all-important commandment to love God and others. We need to allow God's enlivening and transfiguring love to live in us.

Psychological researchers found the importance of love re-confirmed towards the end of WW II. When the air raids began in London, many babies were sent away from their parents, into the countryside where they would be safe from the bombing, the daily noise, and the threats of the Blitz. The infants were housed in institutions where they received state-of-the-art physical care. And yet many of those babies failed to thrive. John Bowlby and other researchers have explored the importance of a loving attachment and have concluded that such an attachment is essential in order for us to grow into healthy, happy people. Love is not a luxury; it is key to our survival.

Our bodies are changed and strengthened when we experience love. When we see or think of someone or something we love, our face usually changes. Eyes soften, a smile forms. For some years, neuroscientist Dr. Steven W. Porges has been studying the myelinated vagus nerve, which links the face, voice, and ear with the heart, lungs, and gut. He has found that those smiles and soft eyes trigger the vagus nerve, with the result that the heart rate and breathing are slowed. The body feels more relaxed. Many other researchers have found that feeling love lowers blood pressure and increases immune functioning.

And – although you might not believe it from observing your love-struck teen – at Rutgers

University, researchers have discovered that love creates focused attention, motivation to successfully complete tasks, and increased energy, along with that feeling of exhilaration.

"God is love. Those who abide in love abide in God, and God abides in them" (1 John 4:16). Although love is certainly a feeling, it is much more than that. In its multi-hued expression, it is the very in-dwelling of the holy – allowing God's power to heal and grow us physically, mentally, emotionally, and spiritually.

HELPING CHILDREN

1. Tell "love" stories. Remember times in your life when you were transfigured, or when someone reached out to you in love. Sharing these stories can reawaken feelings of loving deeply, bringing the same physical benefits to the teller and the listener as the "do-er." It will also teach us to be more aware of love experiences in our current life.

2. Ask children, "How would you show someone you loved them without saying a word?" Write a list

together or draw pictures of examples. The responses from children are usually copious, from cuddling to giving a gift. A link can then be made to the many ways God has shown and continues to show love to each of us.

3. Attributes of God Exercise (adapted from Nancy's book *A Match Made in Heaven: A Bible-based guide to deepening our relationship with God*). As a family or group, ask, "What are some of the things about God that you love?" Answers may range from "God gave us animals, water, sunshine, Jesus" to "God is forgiving and faithful," or God "comforts us when life is hard." As a group, choose seven answers. Each day for a week, pick one of the answers and keep it in mind, looking for "clues" of that thing, which you as a family or group love about God. The evening dinner table or a quiet time before bed can be a good time to share your findings.

4. Notice and gently acknowledge times when children demonstrate or experience deep love. When

you notice a glowing face, you may say, "Thank you for the drawing. And thank you for your love." "I can see how much you love your teacher."

5. Jean Vanier defines Communion as "the to-and-fro of love." We can speak of the Eucharist as a love feast, as a gift given to us in love, and an experience that shows in so many ways that we are loved. You might ask, "During Mass, when were you reminded of God's love?" Remember to share your own experiences.

"In the beginning was the Word. And the Word was with God and the Word was God" (John 1:1). In ancient times, virtually all information was shared orally – not written – and so a "word" never existed apart from a human being who spoke it. It was always an event that took place, an embodied thing, that which existed in the heart and mind, and was given voice. So what was the Word of God? Not: "God had something to say and sent someone to say it." Rather, it literally means that the Love that is the heart of the Creator was given a body to inhabit and live among us. If we were Ents, that would take a long time to say. It's taking God forever.

Song and Resource References

"i hav luv," Linnea Good and Patrick Jonsson-Good, from Linnea Good's CD *Swimmin' Like a Bird*.

CHAPTER 9

A GRATITUDE BEATITUDE

"Hey, Mom, thanks for getting my gym stuff ready!" says ten-year-old Kayla, as she plunks down at the breakfast table.

Mother replies:

A) *Sigh...* "Well, if I didn't, you were going to be late for school."

B) "No problem; that's what parents do."

C) "You're welcome, sweetie. I appreciate you noticing."

Psychologists have been studying gratitude and discovering that giving and receiving thanks is good for us. The experience of receiving gratitude can result in many benefits ranging from heightening our sense of well-being, to lowering our blood pressure, to improving our sleep. A 2008 research project showed that grateful children have more positive attitudes toward school and their families. Studies have shown that, when someone does a good deed for another person, endorphins (hormones of happiness) are released in the giver's brain. They are also released in the brain of the receiver. It may come as a surprise that they are even released in the brain of any onlookers! The attitude and practice of gratitude will further the health of everyone involved.

In Nancy's counselling practice with grieving adults and children, she finds that people often feel the beginnings of healing when they experience gratitude for the support they have received. And of course, many spiritual guides have told us and have demonstrated that being grateful deepens our faith.

On the other hand, negating someone's gratitude – such as Kayla's mother might unwittingly have done in the first two sample responses above – does not let the person experience the full effects of being grateful. It also robs Mom of the full effect of receiving Kayla's gratitude.

Why do we respond to gratitude by saying, "Oh, it's no trouble," or "It was fun," or "Don't mention it"? Apparently, receiving expressions of gratitude makes us uncomfortable. Adults tell us that they sometimes equate saying, "You're welcome," with bragging. However, to "brag" means to overinflate our achievements. We are certainly not doing that when we acknowledge that we have helped someone. In fact, we are being given the opportunity to move into gratitude to God and to ourselves for our ability to be of assistance.

God, knowing how important this spiritual practice is to our faith, encouraged the spiritual guides who developed the content and flow of Mass to include many opportunities to feel and express gratitude. Last Sunday, as Nancy clapped with the rest to show gratitude to the young adults who were music ministers that week, she thought, "Eucharist is truly a wonderful training ground for gratitude."

HELPING CHILDREN

1. Be a "grateful" role model. Be open in your gratitude toward God and people.

2. Thank children for doing their chores.

3. Begin intercessions with gratitude. It produces a very different "heart and mind" when we say,

"Oh, God, I want to tell you my problem and I hope you will help me," than when we pray, "Thank you, God, for what you have been doing about this problem before I even knew it existed. Thank you for what you are doing now and will do in the future. I wish to be more aware of your guidance and support."

4. Shift gratitude from a duty to a pleasure: "I guess I better thank Helen for feeding the cat while we were on holiday" becomes "I'm very grateful that Helen looked after the cat. I want to make her a thank you card. Who wants to help?"

5. Make a Family Gratitude book and encourage all members to draw or write in it when they wish. Watch that this does not become a duty.

6. Ask "What are we grateful for?" at various times during the week – at a meal time, before going to bed, driving to or from church, during a walk in the woods.

7. Involve children in creating or finding different "graces" to say before eating. The first time 4-year-old Isaiah was asked if he wanted to say a grace, he enthusiastically nodded, threw his hands in the air, and yelled, "Thaaaaanks, GOD!!" Searching out graces from other countries or other parts of our own country can help us feel even more connected to God, who loves the whole world.

8. Ask: "What are your favourite thanksgiving hymns?" Sing them. Write and sing your own.

9. Try a gratitude exercise, which helps explore how our own experience of gratitude differs from, or is similar to, that of others. Nancy asks participants to close their eyes and think of a person for whom they feel grateful. She then invites them to reflect on the following questions silently: Where do I experience gratitude in my body? Is it in all parts of me or just in my heart, my stomach, or somewhere else? When I think of gratitude, does a colour come to mind? a particular fragrance? Is gratitude warm or cool? Is it rough or smooth? Does it move or is it still?

Then she continues: "However you experience gratitude, send it out as a blessing to the person you are thinking of. Now, remember others who have helped you in the past and send your gratitude to them. Don't just remember people; animals may have helped you. Certain places may be cause for gratitude." Nancy then gives participants time to do this remembering. Afterwards, she invites people to share their experiences.

Sometimes we need reminders to feel grateful. The greeting card industry has put much time and energy into reminding us to express gratitude and love to others when birthdays, anniversaries, and other special occasions draw near. Holy days and seasons are also opportunities for deepened appreciation. But really, we don't need – and shouldn't wait for – a special occasion. We can express gratitude to God and to all those who share our lives anytime, anyplace. With the benefits going out to all who give, all who receive, and all who are nearby, gratitude truly is the gift that keeps on giving.

Song and Resource References

"It Would've Been Enough," Linnea Good, from her CD *Momentary Saints*.

CHAPTER 10

OBEDIENCE

Once there was a woman with two children. One day, the woman went to the first child and said, "Please tidy up the living room." The child said, "I will," but she played a video game instead. The woman said to her second child, "Please tidy up the living room." The second child said, "I won't." But in a while, he got up and cleaned the room. Now, which of those children did the will of her mother? (adapted from Matthew 21:28–31)

When asked what qualities we would like our children to have, "obedience" might be in the Top 10 for many parents. An obedient child is a happy child — one who has good self-esteem, takes personal responsibility, is becoming self-reliant, and works well with others. An obedient adult is one who respects the laws and rules we live by together, is attuned to the needs of her neighbour, and understands the *"spirit of the law,"* which in turn makes it possible for him or her to make moral decisions.

Obedience is not merely "submission." Sometimes people have been expected to "obey" others blindly and without question: Women have been expected to "obey" men, aboriginals to "obey" European authorities, children to "obey" all adults, welfare recipients to "obey" the "rules." We do not wish for the kind of obedience that diminishes, but rather for a cooperation that teaches responsibility, teamwork, and a sense of attachment to those with authority.

Obedience is love

A variation of the word "obedience" appears 296 times in the Bible, sometimes associated with the people's need and struggle to obey God and, in the gospels, most frequently to describe Jesus' power and relationship with God: the winds and waters obey him, the unclean spirits obey him, he obeys the word of God.

However, obedience is no simple matter. Often, Jesus' opponents try to snare him with moral dilemmas that pit obedience of various kinds or to various "authorities" against each other. "Tell us then," they would ask, "is it right to pay taxes to Caesar or not?" In effect, "To whom are you obedient – to the occupying forces or to the temple?"

Jesus' response about obedience is mixed. In the living room parable, above, obedience means complying with our parent by our actions, not just words. Yet, in another parable, the son who was always obedient is upset because the disobedient one – the prodigal – is welcomed home with rejoicing.

Jesus knew that obedience is not a rote response to a command – simply doing what we are told. *Obedience is a response of love and trust.* When we love someone, we naturally want to do things to please them. When we fear someone, we may obey in order not to be punished, but our obedience will not help us understand *why* we should obey, or assist our reasoning in other situations. Healthy obedience is one way of living the Greatest Commandment – to love God with our whole being, and our neighbour as our self.

Obedience is understanding

Children grow in their ability to be obedient as they develop the capacity to reason and understand.

Part of developing good self-esteem and a feeling of security in the world involves testing limits and encountering consequences of behaviour. Sometimes children, consciously or unconsciously, disobey one directive in order to obey another. It is only with maturity that all implications of a situation can be taken into consideration. With maturity, the older person may still disobey one directive, such as stopping at a red light, in order to obey another directive, getting to the hospital quickly with a wounded child. But with maturity, the person drives carefully through the red light, making sure that everyone involved is safe.

Children are not able to see or understand the wider implications of their actions. Take, for example, the pre-teen who disobeyed his parents' directive to stay close to them as they walked home after a celebration. For three days, the boy was considered lost by his parents. After a frantic search, they discovered him sitting in the temple talking with a group of adults about God. When his mother said to him, "Child, why have you treated us like this? Look, your father and I have been searching for you in great anxiety," Jesus responded with typical pre-adolescent insouciance: "Why were you searching for me? Didn't you know that I must be in my Father's house?"

We love to hear how, from an early age, Jesus was passionate about God. Yet, if we had been Mary or Joseph, we would probably have grounded the boy! This story, in Luke 2, continues: "Then he went down with them and came to Nazareth, and was obedient to them... And Jesus increased in wisdom and in years, and in divine and human favour." So even Jesus had to learn that many factors need to be taken into account in order to discern what is required to be truly obedient in any given situation.

Obedience is deep listening

The quality of obedience has always been important in the Christian tradition as a way of growing in faith, humility, and patience, to name just a few of the traditional Christian virtues. A vow of obedience, along with that of poverty and chastity, is one that men and women have taken for centuries, and continue to take when they enter religious communities, but it is not in any way an extinction of all individuality. Religious obedience does not control the conscience.

The root of "obedience" is *ob-audiere*, which means to "listen attentively." So obedience is about receptivity. Fr. Diarmuid O'Murchu, in his book *Poverty, Celibacy and Obedience: A radical option for life*, says authentic obedience "requires a radical and attentive openness to the deeper message and meaning of all that we are asked to attend to." It requires an openness to hearing from God and using all our faculties to respond in partnership.

Parenting styles and obedience
Research shows that the kind of parenting style that best helps children be attentive to God and to the needs of the world can be termed "moderate authoritative" – the "Backbone" parent (Barbara Coloroso, *Kids Are Worth It!*). These parents live the qualities they want their children to develop. They are clear about limits, explain reasons for their directives, and they realize that children's periodic disobedience is natural. By contrast, the strict authoritative

(Brick Wall) parent makes it harder for children to think for themselves, breeds poor self-esteem, and compliance based on fear. The permissive (Jellyfish) parent does not set limits, which encourages a self-centred, irresponsible – and oftentimes depressed – child.

HELPING CHILDREN

1. Rely on natural consequences as much as possible. This conversation between ten-year-old Emma and her mom is probably familiar.

   "Emmie, lunch time!"

   "But I haven't finished tidying my room yet! Could I still go to the movie this afternoon and do my room later?"

   "Honey, what was our agreement this morning?"

   "We agreed that if I finished my room before lunch, I could go to the movie. I got busy doing other stuff."

   "Then, there is no movie this afternoon."

   (Cry of protest.)

   "I know you're disappointed about the movie,

Emmie. When you're ready, let's decide on a new agreement for another time."

It is okay for Emma to be upset, angry, sad about her consequence. When she is feeling that way, it is not productive to either continue to talk about the consequence, which would feel like "rubbing it in" to Emma, or to attempt to work out a new agreement at that time.

2. Be willing to negotiate and listen to your child's point of view.

3. Pick your conflicts. Sometimes a behaviour changes for the better when ignored.

4. It is usually more effective to support and reward positive behaviour than to focus on negative behaviour.

5. Try to use "No" infrequently. Children tend to tune out a "No" – and it doesn't show them options. Rather than saying, " No, you can't go to Jason's house," say, "Let's make a plan with Ja-

son's mom for you to have a visit when it's not soccer day."

While the word "obedience" may actually have had its day, what it points to is our wish that our children grow in trust of their elders, an intuition for their own inner authority, a deep listening to God, and a desire to find their place contributing positively to their society.

Song and Resource References
"Let the Children Come to Me," Linnea Good, from her CD *Swimmin' Like a Bird*.

CHAPTER 11

PATIENCE

"Are we *there* yet...?"
"I just can't wait for my birthday!"
"I want it NOW!"

Patience is a virtue – and definitely one with which children need help. Some of us grownups do, too! To learn patience, we need to understand what it is as well as some common misunderstandings about it. Then, we can explore some attitudes and behaviours that encourage the growth of patience.

What patience is not
Patience is not "putting ourselves on hold" until an anticipated event occurs. Some people stay in unsatisfying or even abusive situations, such as a relationship or a job, because they feel that they are practicing the virtue of patience. This is not patience; this is "martyred enduring." Unfortunately, to live in either of these ways – "on hold" or "mar-

tyred enduring" – can also mean that the people involved become disengaged from God and are not able to take part in God's activity to build the Kingdom in the present moment.

No true virtue will cause us to be diminished or restricted.

What patience is

True patience involves living as fully as we can in the present – even while we anticipate something happening in the future. In home and church, we pray the Lord's Prayer, in which Jesus invites us to ask God only for the bread we need for this day – in other words, to let our present concerns be sufficient for us. Living in this way is a radical form of trust in the Creator.

God is only found in the *present*.

Delayed gratification

An important aspect of patience is delayed gratification. Delayed gratification is the ability to pass up an immediate pleasure or reward in order to gain a greater or better one later. This is a skill that develops with age and practice. Research indicates that if young children learn how to wait for something they like, they are more likely to develop into adolescents who achieve higher marks in school, are more socially competent, and can handle stress and frustration more effectively. Patience is essential in order to learn anything with a number of steps or with many aspects to it – from getting along with others, to adopting a new spiritual practice, to mastering algebra, to reading a map, to managing our eating.

Ambiguity

Another important aspect of patience is the ability to live with ambiguity. Living with ambiguity refers to the ability to see the grey areas, to understand situations that might have more than one meaning, without needing to know which meaning is the "right" one. Much of life is ambiguous, without a clear-cut "right" way. Ambiguity actually brings richness to life; it is a gift that comes with maturity, helping us to understand the vastly varied experiences and perspectives of others.

Consider the homily you hear in church on Sunday mornings. As part of his preparation and writing during the days prior to Sunday, the priest prays about what he might say in the homily. As he opens to the guidance of the Holy Spirit, the priest can discern a message and meaning that the congregation needs to hear. Yet that same Spirit guides each listener to her or his own meaning as they receive it! So the gospel story may have as many meanings as there are listeners. Those people who are not willing to live patiently – in ambiguity – until the Spirit speaks will take one meaning only for all time from the scripture. An opportunity to grow in faith and closeness with God will be missed. Fr. Anthony de Mello has this to say about patience and ambiguity: "Some people will never learn anything because they grasp too soon. Wisdom, after all, is not a station you arrive at, but a manner of traveling... To know exactly where you're headed may be the best way to go astray. Not all who loiter are lost."

Let's face it; nobody learns patience by hearing somebody talk about it. Children learn what they experience. Our faster-paced culture has caused us to view time as something to be "spent" or "filled." It is hard to learn the art of patience when you are always headed for the next activity.

HELPING CHILDREN

1. Have designated times for certain activities, rather than non-stop access. Make a routine snack time mid-morning and mid-afternoon, rather than allow unsupervised grazing. Decide on a time for TV and video games and then turn them off.

2. Make sure there is enough "down time" in your child's and your own day. Allow fallow time when nothing is programmed and the easy satisfactions are not accessible. When your child says, "I'm bored...," consider it a success – an important moment in which they will need to use their creativity to think of the next possibility.

3. Support make-believe play. Research shows that when children create games, delayed gratification is encouraged. The process of developing characters, roles, activities, etc., takes time, which builds patience.

4. Leave yourself sufficient time to arrive slowly to family functions. Responding to a child's tardiness in a patient way might look like this: "Kylie, we'll be ready to leave in five minutes. What do you still need to do so you can be ready too?" (Kylie answers.) "Okay, buddy, it looks like you have too many things to do with too little time. Let's see what we can change or do later, so we're all ready together."

5. Being told to "just be patient" doesn't really work for most of us. Help children to live in the present. Isaac says, "When Matthew comes, it's going to be awesome, Mom! Why do we have to wait two whole hours?!" A possible response: "I know you are really looking forward to his visit, Isaac. What would be fun to do while you're waiting?"

6. Teach patience in steps. For example, the Ortiz family has a tradition of completing a jigsaw puzzle over the holidays. The first few years, each puzzle had few pieces, so the project could be completed over 3 or 4 days, taking the preschool attention span into account. As the children grew in their ability to be patient, subsequent years involved more complex scenes, with many more pieces.

7. Show children your own challenges and successes with being patient. "My goodness, it's hard for me to wait for our camping trip. Today I caught myself daydreaming about the lake, rather than working. I prayed, 'God, help me to enjoy the present,' and then I found it easier to focus on the work I was doing."

To a certain extent, the practice of patience is an expression of our letting go of control over details — not sweating the small stuff. For us adults, perhaps it involves releasing some of the micro-managing and micro-worrying we do. This is difficult when we wish to be "competent" caregivers. However, the patience we show to ourselves and to our children will go a long way toward fostering that same virtue in our young.

Have patience
with everything that lies upon your heart.
Unresolved.
Try to love the questions for themselves
Don't go searching for the answers which could not be given now
Don't go chasing after reasons when in truth you don't know how

Just have patience
For somewhere far beyond you, you might see
step by step
little by little
though your spirit scarcely marks the changes past
you'll have lived your life
into
the thing you asked.

– words adapted from Rainer Maria Rilke's
Letters to a Young Poet
by Linnea Good in the song "Patience," from her CD
Momentary Saints

Song and Resource References

"Patience," words adapted from Rainer Maria Rilke by Linnea
Good, from her CD *Momentary Saints.*

CHAPTER 12

MORE THAN FAIR

Once there was a woman who was rich – at least in all the ways that mattered most: she had family, friends, food on the table, and meaning in her work. Cash she had not much; it had been a tough year for work. One day, the woman brought her family to a benefit concert for "the poor" in town. She came because her eldest was making his guitar debut on stage – and because, of course, she wanted her family to contribute to "the poor."

At the door, she asked the ticket takers if there was a family rate for tickets. They replied in confusion that, no, there didn't seem to be one and, no, they couldn't make an exception because they were only volunteers. They pointed to the person in charge. The mother approached this woman and asked her if an exception might be made to the single ticket rule, as it would have been a bit of a hardship to the family to pay in this way. Glancing in at the roomful of people in theatre seats, the woman replied slowly that she couldn't make an exception because "those people in there might have liked to have a break in the price, too, but they didn't get one." The mother sighed and said, "I just wonder if you might be able to be flexible with the price; it's been... a bit of a year." The door manager said, "It wouldn't be fair for me to give something to *you* that I have not offered to others." To this she added, "It *is* to raise money for the poor, you know..."

The mother knew that this was the moment to go home, to not make a fuss and a scene. But the family *had* to attend; the eldest boy was performing that night. Taking a deep breath, she said, "There is something I think you don't understand. THIS is what it looks like when someone comes to you who is ..." And in that moment, the woman made the decision to cross a line she had never crossed in her life, and in front of her children, she said, "...poor."

The ticket manager's face coloured and, with frustration, she flung back to the ticket sellers, "Give her whatever she wants." And the woman paid a bit less for the tickets. And the family attended the concert. The performance was rich. And her eldest played admirably.

But that woman went home poor.

Fair vs. Just

From an early age, children learn from us that we are to be fair – that everyone deserves the same and no one should be favoured. We teach our children to respect all people as God's beloved, and to show kindness to all, regardless of our differences. The notion of fairness is central to our ability to live together in society. But when is fairness not enough?

Fr. Luigi Taparelli first used the term "social justice" in 1840, basing this concept on the teachings of St. Thomas Aquinas. It is now a foundation of Christian teaching, as well as the teaching of many other faith and secular groups. Social justice generally refers to the idea of creating a society that is based on principles of equality and solidarity, and that values human rights and the dignity of every human being.

Social fairness, on the other hand, refers to being impartial or non-preferential. People often focus more on impartiality when being fair. Impartial means "having no direct involvement or interest and not favouring one person or side more than another."

Fairness means that everyone has access to the same resources: air, water, respect, health care, school, etc. Justice means that some are able to contribute *more*; others *need* more and receive more because of it.

To this, Jesus added another layer. To those who said, "If people are poor, it is their own fault," Jesus replied, "Blessed are the poor, for God's kingdom is theirs." To those who said, "If people are sick or grieving, it is because God is punishing them with misfortune," he replied, "Blessed are those who mourn, for they shall be comforted." To the scales of fairness, Jesus added the balance of "grace." God *especially* cares for those who are down, sick, poor, in need. God's Spirit is poured out, *especially* so on those who need it the most.

When we are attached to the notion that all should be treated in exactly the same way, we risk missing the very real needs of others around us. It becomes necessary to carve up the world into the "Haves" and the "Needy." But doing so can do damage to people's dignity in the process. Instead of simply seeing a neighbour who could use a hand, we force that person to become "the Other."

HELPING CHILDREN

1. When speaking with children who have acted in ways that are not just and fair, be a role model for the concepts. Speak with the children in ways that recognize their dignity. Rather than blaming or shaming children, by saying such things as, "That's not nice! Jesus is mad at you!" instead, you might try something like, "Everyone gets a turn at the game. Then let's see who wants to go a second time."

2. The heat of the moment is not the best time for long explanations, so we might talk about how members of groups, such as families, look at the special needs of each person: "Your dad and I know that younger children need more sleep to help them grow, and that is why you and your sister have different bedtimes."

3. To explore this concept more fully with older children and teens, read the Parable of the Workers in the Vineyard (Matthew 20:1–20):

For the kingdom of heaven is like a landowner who went out early in the morning to hire labourers for his vineyard. The landowner came to an agreement with some labourers for the wage to be paid them and they started at 9 a.m. Later, others were asked to work as well and some started work at noon, others at 3 and 5 p.m. At the end of the day all received the same amount.

Ask the youth to choose identities for the ones who came late and to give reasons for why the workers might have done so: for example, "I'm a single mom on social assistance and had to get the kids off to school, then walk to the grocery store because I don't have a car, and then walk to the place where they were hiring. I got there at noon."

When the ones who had been working all day complained, the landowner replied, "Am I not allowed to do what I choose with what belongs to me? Are you jealous because I am generous?"

"What does the Holy One require of you but to do justice, and to love kindness, and to walk humbly with your God?" It is much "easier" to be fair than to be "just," because being just takes more thought and widens our perception of a situation. There are no easy answers. When we understand our lives to be full and meaningful, we experience God's generosity not as something that steals scarce resources, but as something that allows everyone to share in earth's rich abundance. Such an expansive shift in perspective may be exactly what this world needs at this critical time.

Song and Resource References

"The Way It Should Be," Linnea Good, from her CD *Sunday Sessions.*

CHAPTER 13

AWE

Stevie let the screen door slam behind him as he pelted into the kitchen. "Mom, Dad — it's awesome! Come and look!"

Stevie's dad looked up from the carrots he was chopping. "Hey, buddy, what's awesome?"

The boy called, "There's a double rainbow out there! The whole sky is full of it!"

Mom had already left the oven to follow him outside. The three stared in awe for a while and then Stevie whispered, "Fr. Frank says the rainbow is a promise that God made to us, to love us forever. So this is like a double promise." As the family returned to the house, Dad said to Stevie, "Thanks for sharing that with us."

Although the word "awesome" is most often used today to refer to something that is "really good," the original meaning of "awe" is much richer. *The Oxford American Dictionary* defines awe as "a feeling of reverential respect mixed with fear or wonder."

In their book *Gifts of the Eucharist,* Nancy and Bernadette Gasslein suggest that a young child's innate sense of wonder is possibly more fully expressed than an adult's. "An experience moves out of the ordinary and elicits feelings of awe when we give our full attention to it. Have you ever idly watched a butterfly and then suddenly become aware of a child's rapt attention to the fluttering insect? The child's connection to the butterfly is so full that the result is awe, while you only experience mild enjoyment."

The more of ourselves we give to an experience, the more we are likely to receive from it. Jesus told his followers, "Pay attention to what you hear; the measure you give will be the measure you get, and still more will be given you" (Mark 4:24).

The fear of God

Awe is the experience that is meant when the phrase "fear of the Lord" is used in scripture. When we live the first commandment – loving God with our body, mind, heart, and spirit – we develop a deeper sense of awe, with its mixture of fear and wonder. At times we will experience wonder and at other times fear.

The fear, though, is not of God's actions; the fear arises when we perceive a threat to our status quo, or existing state. When an overwhelming experience washes over us, we become aware that it could carry us away – into unknown emotional terrain, into huge realizations, into newness and change. Part of us does not want to change. Another part of us, however, realizes that the divine invitation is to become a new creation, refined and transformed by love. Indeed, every time we take the "bread of life" and every time we drink the "cup of blessing" in Communion, God invites us to die and rise again with Jesus.

The flash of fear that comes with awe can help us realize how precious God is to us. It reminds us that God has relinquished power over us by giving us free will. Our lives belong to us as a gift. We are loved so much that we have the freedom to accept or reject God's invitation to refinement and transformation. However, the fear becomes unhealthy if we don't allow it to transform into wonder. Living in fear binds and diminishes us, keeping our focus on our weaknesses and faults. Indeed, every time we receive Christ's Body and Blood, God invites us to die and rise again with Jesus. We attend Mass, not as beloved children giving thanks for the gift of Jesus and of God's love, but often condemning and judging ourselves in anticipation of an even greater judgment, which we fear will come at the hands of a vindictive God. This not only harms our self-esteem, it distorts the reality of God.

Awe is awesome

A column in the February 9, 2010, issue of *The New York Times* was entitled "Will You Be E-Mailing This Column? It's Awesome." The article concerned research out of the University of Pennsylvania conducted by Jonah Berger and Katherine A. Milkman. Over a six-month period, the researchers analyzed which articles from *The New York Times* had been shared via e-mail most frequently. Tracking over 7,500 articles, they found that the ones shared most frequently had the same characteristic: they offered readers an experience of awe. In the words of Dr. Berger, it was "that awed feeling that the world is a broad place and I'm so small." The researchers defined awe as an "emotion of self-transcendence, a feeling of admiration and elevation in the face of something greater than the self." To test whether a story was awe-inspiring, the researchers looked for a "grand scale" and one that necessitated "mental accommodation" – looking at the world in a different way.

HELPING CHILDREN...and Ourselves

Stevie, seeing the double rainbow, runs to share the experience with his parents. Thousands of adult readers of an awe-inspiring article e-mail it to their friends. Because the experience of awe strongly encourages us to change, broaden our horizons, and see the Holy more fully in our day-to-day existence, we may be tempted to water down the experience or laugh at children's "innocence." Yet children often do not have the ego issues about feeling "small," "overwhelmed," or "not in control" that concern many adults. We can help children to retain this ability to experience awe by honouring their experience, by giving words to it and, if invited, by sharing our own experiences with them.

In fact, children have much to teach adults in this area of faith. Time spent with young ones can allow us to grow in our ability to see the world as others see it and to be blessed with new vision. The most important thing we adults can do for ourselves and for our children is to allow ourselves to have the experience of awe more frequently. We can let the Holy Spirit, and our children, help us. We can let ourselves feel very small compared to the infinity of God. We can allow ourselves to be overwhelmed by the love this God has for us. And we can realize that we do not control our lives, our children, the universe, or our God.

And let's take the time to nurture our own sense of awe about our children. The busy-ness that overflows our days can make us impatient or unaware of their incredible uniqueness. When the day threatens to become just a series of checklists to fill out, may we take a breath before we speak – and say a silent word of thanks to God for their existence in our lives. Awe can change everything.

Song and Resource References

"It's a Wonder," Linnea Good, from her CDs *Sometimes Christmas* and *Greatest of These.*

CHAPTER 14

O GREAT EARTH

In the crackling cold of a northern midnight, Jill's parents awakened her, leading her out by moonlight into the backyard. There the aurora borealis was in full, soaring flight. "As we watched the lights dance," says Jill, "Mom whispered, 'Thank you, God, for giving us such a beautiful world.' I began a thank you dance and my parents joined in. Until I became a teenager, our family would often do that thank you dance whenever we encountered some new aspect of God's gifts."

When we ask adults to remember experiences of the sacred in their childhood, they frequently speak of times when they met God in creation.

"I often felt awe and wonder while watching a sunset."

"There was a special tree on the farm. I'd climb onto 'my' branch, where I'd have a deep sense of security and of being loved. I called it the 'God tree.'"

"Lying on the prairie, gazing into the endless

sky, often gave me a sense of being 'one' with all creation, that God loved every created thing, and I felt great joy. That experience was my prayer time."

"Gardening with dad was a special time in my childhood. He explained how we are stewards of the earth."

Soaking in God's creation

All of creation is telling the glory of God. The earth, the water, the trees, and the creatures resound with a holy Sabbath hymn. Studies have found that just being outdoors is health-giving; yet fewer and fewer children have the opportunity to simply "be" in touch with the earth, as we increasingly become urban dwellers. Yet, once made, the transition to being with the earth is one that we cannot imagine undoing. Here are some suggestions to consider when planning time that is deep in experiences of Earth.

Go outside and play

A repeated refrain among the parents of our generation, "Go outside and play!" is less frequently heard in North American homes these days. Perhaps we are more anxious about our children's safety outdoors (although crimes against young people have actually decreased in the last decades). Perhaps we worry our children are already overprogrammed. Perhaps we are too easily seduced by the easy childcare offered by television and electronics. Yet ecologists such as Richard Louv, author of *Last Child in the Woods: Saving Our Children from Nature-Deficit Disorder*, remind us that there are strong links between spending time in the natural world and children's ability to learn, their physical well-being, and their emotional health. Stress levels, attention-deficit hyperactivity disorder, brain abilities, and more are all positively affected by spending time in nature.

Send children outdoors every day. Because children benefit from simply being outdoors and because the unstructured, unplanned environment of kid-play develops imagination and co-operative social skills, there is no need to send them with directions or equipment. They will find their own activity.

Limit the use of electronics

We suggest setting a limit on children's use of electronics – not because electronics are bad, but because our job as parents is to help our children develop their many God-given gifts and abilities. The skills enriched by video games and computer activities encourage particular kinds of thinking. Most particularly, however, gaming and TV-watching eat up a whole lot of time. Time spent outdoors pays back in dividends. Set a limit for daily "screen-time," which might include – and require children to choose between – the various games and shows available to them. Then send them outdoors.

Go camping

Spend time away from the city lights. Bring as little "stuff" as you can. Do nothing. Let the campfire be your devotion. See what happens.

Send children to camp

Many churches run summer camp programs that offer profound experiences of self and nature. Their mix of faith exploration, games and activities, crafts, music, and the natural world creates life-long memories.

Go on everyday pilgrimages

People undertake pilgrimages to places such as Lourdes with the hope of healing, guidance, or a conversion experience. Although the site is a holy one, it is not only the destination itself that holds the promise of God's presence and power. In fact, pilgrims may receive guidance, healing, insight – and any other gift – on the journey. God is found in our present, not in the idea of our future. So it is helpful to practice the discernment skills of receptivity, listening, attention, and gratitude during all parts of the pilgrimage. All these can be practiced in an everyday pilgrimage.

An everyday pilgrimage may have a body of water, a forest, a bird sanctuary, a city park, or your own backyard as a destination. Start the pilgrimage with prayer, asking God for suggestions on the destination; discuss any "urgings" or "nudges" that have come. Undertake all parts of the journey – preparing food, dressing, putting on sunscreen, etc.

– with the gentle awareness that God is present. Walk or ride the path with love and gratitude. Enjoy the gift of creation. Do not rush, direct, or judge the experience. Share highlights or learnings when you return home.

HELPING CHILDREN

1. Share your own experiences of God in creation. Thank God out loud.

2. Listen when children speak of awe or wonder in nature.

3. Pray with children, giving thanks for nature, and for the parts that need healing and care, asking God to show you how you can be part of the healing.

4. Garden indoors or outdoors with your child. Take some of the produce to a local food bank or neighbour.

5. Go on a scavenger hunt, looking for objects that have various characteristics: e.g., bumpy, rough, smooth, yellow, fragrant. If it would not harm

the object to bring it home, have the child do so. Otherwise, the child can record it in words or as a drawing.

6. Do volunteer work with your child or join an organization that helps the natural world.

7. Drive into the country at least a few times to purchase food directly from farmers at roadside stands, or pick produce yourself. Talk with the farmer(s). Talk with children about how different the land looks each time, with its different crops, colours, etc.

O Great Earth so green and so blue
This is the promise that I make to you
To care for your children, for children can hear
the rhythm of your heartbeat.

– "O Great Earth" by Linnea Good, from her CD

Swimmin' Like a Bird

Song and Resource References

"O Great Earth," Linnea Good, from her CD *Swimmin' Like a Bird*.

Hurst, Viki. *Personal Pilgrimage: One Day Soul Journeys for Busy People*. Kelowna, BC: Northstone Publishing, 2001. (Northstone Publishing is an imprint of Wood Lake Publishing Inc.)

CHAPTER 15

MY LIFE FLOWS ON IN ENDLESS SONG

It was at the "memorial service" for my daughter's dog, Amber, says Nancy. Six-year-old Christina and a number of her peers had just planted some spring bulbs in the backyard. "The flowers should be the colour of Amber's fur," said 8-year-old Maggie, who had taken charge of the proceedings. "Now we can look at pictures and remember Amber, and then have the cake. But first we have to sing a hymn." The children, looking very solemn, nodded and turned to me: "What's a good hymn for a dog?" I thought fast but couldn't come up with even one suggestion. Maggie stepped in. As she began to sing, the others joined in, happily and reverently...

"There was a girl who had a dog
and Amber was her name-o
A*M*B*E*R!
A*M*B*E*R!
A*M*B*E*R!
And Amber was her name-o"

As I joined in the singing, I watched the kids glow with anticipation as each letter in AMBER was changed to a clap. When the song finished, I could see that their mood had changed. There were more smiles as they filed into the house to look at the photograph albums. Christina's buddy, Scott, smiled: "Good hymn."

Have you ever found that music has lifted your mood or moved you into a more reverent feeling? Do you have favourite phrases that you just can't wait to get to when the hymn starts? Recently, researchers at McGill University have discovered that anticipating a favourite part of music causes an increase in the neurotransmitter dopamine. Increased dopamine produces a strong positive emotional response – a euphoria – that often brings a physical sensation of "chills." Other research shows an increase in dopamine when people look at photos of their beloved, or when they are deep in prayer or meditation. It is not hard to see that singing can create a state that allows people to be receptive to God.

Singing also *grows* our brain. It encourages both sides of the brain to work in tandem, which in turn helps our thinking become more integrated in various skill areas. It is a way of hearing – of perceiving and understanding.

"Those who sing, pray twice," wrote St. Augustine. It is the rare child who doesn't sing, naturally and spontaneously. Through music, children express love, gratitude, awe, sadness, anger, and every other emotion known to humankind. In fact, music often helps children express feelings and concerns they could not find words for. By listening to a child humming or singing, an adult can often tell how that child is feeling.

Charlotte Diamond, educator, musician, composer and president of Hug Bug Music Canada says, "Music, singing, and movement are a major part of a child's early development. The most wonderful sound in a preschool is the gentle humming of children as they play or draw. They freely experiment with the sound of their own voices, singing for the love of it. They communicate that joy to themselves and to others around them, vibrating with a natural spirituality. We feel more complete when we sing or play music. By releasing our emotions and creativity, we are connected to something much greater than ourselves. The troubled times that we face in our lives are diminished when our days are sprinkled with moments of musical fun and joy. The song is just the beginning!"

Stephen Fischbacher is the Creative Director of Fischy Music, a UK-based charity that promotes the emotional and spiritual well-being of children through music. The charity goes into churches and schools, touching the lives of thousands of children each year. Stephen has written that music helps children in their spiritual growth by creating a sense of belonging to the group – empowering each child, since all types of voices are needed – and by connecting them to a world beyond the here-and-now and present circumstances.

Similarly, The Saint James Academy in Vancouver, located in the lowest income neighbourhood in British Columbia, has as their mission statement, "Through the inspiration and joy of collaborative music making... we give young people in the Downtown Eastside... the opportunity to explore their creative potential, gain self-confidence, get an academic head start, and become role models within their family and community."

Linnea's experience with music in the church has shown her that children often lead adults in expressing themselves through song. Though we sometimes underestimate or inadvertently undermine the integrity of their participation in worship by laughing at their "cuteness," children show considerable honesty when they sing their faith with us; we could learn much from them.

Years ago, Linnea found some words typed on her computer by her then-4-year-old son, Patrick: "I hav luv and mi hos dos to." Though he didn't know it, Patrick had written a song: "I have love and my house does, too." With his mother's melody, Patrick's words have now become a song that is sung by many people to express the inexpressible of the heart: the love that can live in a family, and the intimacy that can be found in the sanctuary of the church.

HELPING CHILDREN

1. Adults who sing without reserve are more likely to have children who spontaneously do so. Many adults were told as children that they should not sing. As a result, they may feel inhibited about their own musical sound. If that happened to you, give yourself permission to go ahead and make your own music. Sing in the shower, at the stove, during chores, etc. Your own freedom will have a positive influence on those around you, particularly your children.

2. Have music playing in your home some, but not all, of the time. Having music of a variety of styles to accompany your daily life can change the mood of the house and effortlessly teach appreciation of different genres, including the music of faith. However, do leave time for silence (or at least musical and electronic silence) in the home as well, so that your family does not become regularly shut-down to sounds from outside.

3. When parishes use a variety of styles of music in worship, children learn to express themselves in different ways. When hymns and songs of faith are sung in both traditional and contemporary styles, members of the congregation, of all ages, find a place to "be at home." When both abstract and concrete imagery is used, a variety of spiritual styles is honoured.

4. Sing hymns with multiple verses, as well as song refrains that are short and repeated. Sing pieces that invite movement so that the whole body can sing. Sing a spectrum of songs: fast and loud, fun and funny, slow and heartfelt, restrained, uninhibited, anticipatory, prayerful. Allow children the full expression of emotion that you would wish to elicit from adult worshippers.

Music transcends boundaries in the brain, just as it transcends the sometimes-difficult gap between our everyday life and the luminous existence we seek in Christ. It is a powerful spiritual gift, especially so because it is more blessed the more we share in it with others.

i

hav luv

and mi hos dos to

i hav luv and mi hos dos to

There is love under my bed

There is love over my head

i hav luv and mi hos dos to

Song and Resource References

"Stand on the Rock" (Psalm 122), Linnea Good, from her CD *Momentary Saints*.

Salimpoor, Valorie, et al. "Anatomically distinct dopamine release during anticipation and experience of peak emotion to music," in *Nature Neuroscience* (2011).

Fischbacher, Stephen. *Music and Spirituality*. Article at www.docstoc.com/docs/18386584/Music-and-Spirituality.

More information at www.fischymusic.com

CHAPTER 16

LIVING THE CHURCH YEAR

"Hey, Mom!" called seven-year-old Daniel. "Where's our Christ candle?"

When his mother replied that they didn't have one, Daniel was nonplussed. "Why not? We have Advent candles every year. The Christ candle at church is so beautiful. Fr. Jim said we use it in church to show that God is here, right now. So I thought we could light it every day and say a prayer."

Daniel's mother wondered, why not indeed? Celebrating God's presence, especially by recognizing the seasons of the church year, is an experience that can so richly be shared by all ages in the family. A ritual captures a really "big thing" that we want to express in an action that is focused and, usually, repeated. It takes the really "big thing" and deepens it without having to explain it over and over again, allowing us to experience it with our eyes, our ears, our noses, tongues, hands, feet, etc. Every year, worshipping congregations remember some really "big things" together: the birth of Jesus, his resurrection, the many attributes of God, the teaching and healing ministry of Jesus, the sending of the Spirit at Pentecost...

Each season of the church year has its own colour and prayers, as well as emotional and spiritual "flavours" and symbols. Bringing the seasons of the church year into the home invites children into a deeper understanding of their own spiritual experiences, and of the ways in which their religion understands those things. It encourages spiritual practices that all members of the family can express, each in their own way.

Perhaps you already have rituals in your home: grace at a meal, prayers at bedtime, lighting candles on birthdays. Some rituals are traditional, having been passed down through the generations and carried out according to family custom. Other rituals may be unique to your family, perhaps made up in bursts of creativity.

Daniel was seeking to bring the traditional ritual of lighting the Christ candle into his home. His mother might choose to buy one at a Christian book store, or she might simply use a regular white candle.

Other rituals originate from the creativity of family members. As the family drove home from the Pentecost service one year, five-year-old Sarah said, "I'll do some drawings of the Holy Spirit and the people with fire on their heads and we can put them in the dining room for the feast."

"What feast?" asked her older brother. Sarah rolled her eyes. "Weren't you listening in church? This is the feast of Pentecost. We gotta eat!"

Auntie was intrigued. "What kind of food would we have for a Pentecost feast?"

"Fiery, spicy food," said Sarah's brother.

The rest of the ride home was spent in a lively conversation about appropriate feast food for Pentecost. The evening was spent eating it.

Each culture celebrates its own feast days – such as the Mexican "Day of the Dead" (*Dia de los Muertos*) on All Saints' / All Souls' Day. Sugar skulls, marigolds, and visiting cemeteries are all part of this important feast. In Canada, the feast day of John the Baptist is Quebec's national holiday.

HELPING CHILDREN

To create a ritual to mark seasons and occasions in the church year, you might do the following.

1. Stay attuned to what the children are talking about. Catch them where their interest lies. Sarah's auntie knew that she was interested in a feast to celebrate Pentecost at their house, so she asked the next question: What kind of food? The celebration took shape from there.

2. Choose one physical object from the season's key scripture. During Advent, if you have a crèche or nativity scene, you might start the Magi in another room of the house and have them "make their way" toward the stable every week, or even daily. This activity keeps the family focused on the upcoming Holy birth. In Lent (the season of the bare simplicity of spirit), are there stark, desert-like things you could put on display?

3. As a feast day draws near, adults and children can research when and how the particular day

came into being. The family can then discuss the meaning of the day and plan what type of celebration they wish to have. Become clear about the "big thing" you are celebrating. At Pentecost, for example, Sarah's family ate fiery food to remember how passionate and mighty God's Spirit is in our world.

4. Consider which colours to use, display, or wear to help your eyes celebrate.

5. Think about what sounds might help your ears celebrate. Would you like music to be part of this? Will you sing?

6. Help others celebrate. Would you like to invite anyone to attend?

7. Finally, examine what you have created to make sure that the overt message ("big thing") that you are instilling is not undermined by an underlying, less important one. For example, to celebrate the Holy Spirit's unfettered freedom at Pente-

cost with a ritual that is tightly controlled and only allows some people to participate sends, at best, a mixed message. Likewise, attempting to celebrate God's great love for this Earth by using disposable, pollution-producing items is counter-productive.

Bear in mind that children can be huge tradition-alists. Linnea recalls the observation made by her friend the year her family celebrated the children's second and third Christmas together: "Lucky you. You probably have one more Christmas before everything gets cast in stone and you are not allowed to change your practices, ever." It can be helpful to think through what you start, if you have people with good memory and orthodox inclinations in your family.

On the other hand, it can be important to allow a ritual to spring up out of the life of the family. Feel free and enjoy! Celebrations can be as simple as reading a short story about St. Francis on his feast day, sharing around the table what "family" means to each person on Thanksgiving, or

displaying photos and objects on the day of someone's birth, baptism, or death.

The "big things" that the rituals of the church
teach us are so big they are literally impossible to
convey with words. They celebrate that there is
meaning to our existence and that God really wants
us to draw near, receiving guidance and savouring
fullness of life with others on this journey.

Song and Resource References

"Make a Joyful Noise" (Psalm 100), Linnea Good, from her CD
Greatest of These.

Alternatives. *Treasury of Celebrations: Create Celebrations that
Reflect Your Values and Don't Cost the Earth.* Kelowna, BC:
Northstone Publishing, 1996. (Northstone Publishing is an
imprint of Wood Lake Publishing Inc.)

Alternatives. *Simplify and Celebrate: Embracing the Soul of
Christmas.* Kelowna, BC: Northstone Publishing, 1997
(Northstone Publishing is an imprint of Wood Lake
Publishing Inc.)

CHAPTER 17

PREPARING TO CELEBRATE –
WORSHIP THROUGHOUT THE YEAR

"Brianna, GET UP! You'll make us late for Mass!" When 14-year-old Brianna Proctor finally appeared, there was barely time to eat the breakfast her father had prepared. Brianna wolfed hers down and bolted with the others out the door. By the time the four Proctors made it to the church, the congregation was launching into the first hymn.

"Nice you could make it," whispered Brianna's friend Megan, who had been saving them space. Brianna responded with a growl.

Her 18-year-old brother translated: "Mom and Dad are freaking out."

The adult Proctors spent most of Mass looking frazzled.

Preparing to worship
Life is full and in our busy lives it is so easy to view Mass as one more appointment. We arrive, or try to

arrive, on time – in body, but perhaps not in spirit. We may not really think about Mass until we are there. Yet we know that our own readiness makes any event more meaningful. Careful preparation can enhance the experience of Eucharist for our children as well.

HELPING CHILDREN

1. Arrange your timing so that you are not rushing to church. Take a careful look at the real amount of time it takes to get the family out the door. This might mean backing up the "We-are-leaving" deadline or even shifting mealtimes.

2. Many children have difficulty making transitions from one activity to another, especially if it means leaving the premises. Help children make the shift to church by giving them advance notice that you will be leaving in 20, then 10 minutes, etc. You might say, "Caitlin, we'll be leaving in 20 minutes. So please finish the page you're reading and then get ready." Checking on Caitlin in a few

minutes, the parent could either say, "Thank you for putting down your book. When you're ready, please meet us out at the car," or "It looks like that book is really interesting. Where can you put it so that you can find it when we come home from Mass?"

3. Consider making the travel to church (and the church itself) a no-electronics zone. The punchy, instant-gratification mood created by hand-held electronic games may not be conducive to a receptive, worshipful experience.

4. Take a few moments as a family to talk about the upcoming experience, prior to leaving for church. "Sister Connie will be telling a story about Mary today. What do you remember about last week's story about Zechariah?"

Living into the Christmas season
Christmas is coming! Many church school curricula suggest Advent practices such as constructing an Advent wreath, a crib, or Jesse tree; using an

Advent calendar; and choosing cards, gifts, and decorations to reflect the true "reason for the season."

One or more of these practices may be among your cherished family traditions. Sometimes, though, we can become overwhelmed with the busyness and hype that surround Christmas and see these activities as one more chore. These activities, along with attending Christmas Mass, are meant to help us grow closer to God in Jesus. So choose particular Advent rituals carefully, keeping in mind that they need to be done as spiritual practices.

While there is room for Christmas fun that is not "religious" or "spiritual" per se, if you find that you are caught up in so many Santa- or toy-oriented traditions that the real gift of Christmas has become a "frill" or has lost its meaning, you might wish to look at letting go of some of them. Choose with quality, not quantity, in mind.

We suggest that families decide on activities together, talking about what traditional rituals have meant to each person in the past, and what they mean now. God calls us to spiritual practices that will be most beneficial for our growth in faith.

Therefore, over time, as we follow God's guidance, one spiritual practice may replace another. God takes our current needs into account, when inviting us into deeper relationship.

Some families develop new rituals. Take the Proctors: they traditionally woke at 7 a.m., opened presents, ate breakfast, and attended Christmas Mass. This schedule worked well with young children. Waking teenagers at the crack of dawn, however, required explosives. No one wanted to eat before Mass; this resulted in four irritable Proctors attending the service.

The family had a discussion and decided to open presents after Mass and have a leisurely brunch instead. In this way, Christmas day became more spiritual. It took courage for the family to talk about a possible change; but when they came up with a solution they all could live with, their experience of Christmas day was greatly enhanced.

Sometimes we tenaciously hold on to outdated traditions just because "it's always been done that way in our family." However, as Jaroslav Pelikan writes, "Tradition is the living faith of the dead; tra-ditionalism is the dead faith of the living."

Advent

During Advent, the church services remind us that Christ is given to us as a gift entrusted in love. It is easy to get caught up in rituals that symbolize the reverse of this unconditional trust. Many of us over-spend at Christmas, somehow trying to catch up to a set of expectations that we feel we must live up to. Take the time to identify for yourself and with your children what the real blessings of Christmas are (visits with friends, family, songs to sing and other music, special Christmas videos, trimming the tree...). If lowering your overall budget for your Christmas spending does not work for you (compli-cated as that is for many), you might simply imag-ine the "budget size" for the gift you had planned to give to each person and visualize getting something smaller.

Advent and Christmas rituals, as well as other traditions of the Church year, are meant to complement worship and draw us more deeply into our relationship with God. With a little bit of advance thinking, planning and praying, we might find that God manages to break through our busy lives and give us just exactly what we are praying for.

Song and Resource References

"Oh, What a Wonderful Gift," Linnea Good, from her CD *Sometimes Christmas*.

CHAPTER 18

A MISSION FOR ALL AGES

As far as we know, history was made on March 22, 2009 – the first night of the St. Charles parish Lenten Mission. That evening, the Edmonton church filled with both adults and children exploring one theme together: "A Match Made in Heaven – Learning to Love God More Fully."

Parish Missions have traditionally been for adults. A strong tradition in our church, they have offered an important opportunity for Catholics to explore their faith and receive spiritual nurture. It was for precisely this reason that Fr. Frank and the pastoral staff of St. Charles wanted to open their event to a wider body of the congregation. They wanted to broaden the mission for the whole Body of Christ and to "let the children come" – along with the adults.

But how do you adjust an event that has been composed largely of speaking presentations to include children? Would adults feel that there had been enough theological input to satisfy their needs, if children took part? Would children be forced to sit through speaking that went over their heads? Would people come?

The St. Charles staff believed they would. But some things needed to change if the mission were to be open to more – and different kinds of – people. In previous years, the group that came tended to be in the older-adult bracket. A three-evening event was a large commitment and possibly prohibitive for parents of young children. By offering a youth component to the mission, they were also making the event accessible to these younger adults. As well, speaker-oriented events tend to address the faithful in only one learning style. Offering more diverse opening presentations of music, drama, story and prayer addressed a variety of spiritual needs, so that people of all ages could be nurtured. Most importantly, the staff knew that bringing together children, youth, middle adults, and elders created a relationship and dialogue that would deeply enrich the spiritual life of the whole community.

Content and flow

So, in this Mission, children and adults had time together and time apart. In each one-and-a-quarter-hour session, Nancy presented two qualities for deepening a relationship with God, based on her book *A Match Made in Heaven: A Bible-based guide to deepening your relationship with God.* Qualities such as love, self-awareness, gratitude, spiritual discernment, reconciliation and healing, were introduced with songs and stories appropriate for the whole group. The stories for the whole group were parables, gospel stories, or everyday illustrations of Jesus' teachings. Then, Linnea took the children for spiritual activities that explored that quality, while Nancy spoke with the adults.

Our Schedule

5:30–6:15 Potluck dinner

6:30 Mission beginning time (a time that makes it easier for young children and older adults to attend). Full Group: Together in the sanctuary, the group gathers for ten minutes to sing and pray.

A brief thematic presentation is made — ideally in the form cf story or small drama or interactive "scriptural telling."

6:40   Split Age-Groups: Children leave for 30 minutes. Their theme time incorporates group-building, music, movement, story, games, art and optional "centres," such as a prayer corner, drawing, clay, etc. While they do so, a presentation for adults takes place in the main room. While the adults explore possibly two "qualities" each evening, the children focus on one.

7:10   Full Group: Children return for prayer and a song in the large group to close.

7:15   Reception

Considerations when planning an All-Ages Mission
Missions are traditionally held during Advent and Lent. However, poor weather, Christmas preparations, school and parish pageants make the season

sometimes less than ideal for a mission. Some parishes are letting go of the Advent event in favour of a Thanksgiving Mission.

In congregations without an extensive history with all-ages events, it might be helpful to advertise the event as a "regular" parish mission *paired with* a children's mission. While still following the all-ages format, this shift in description might alleviate concerns about the actual focus of the evenings.

Our team chose an "all-ages" rather than "family" focus. In some parishes, a family mission may be preferable. In such an event, children would remain and interact with their adults throughout the evening.

Care should be taken to plan for, and staff, the wide spread of ages that might attend the children's component. It is preferable to have preschoolers, six- to 11-year-olds, and youth in separate modules. And given the interactive nature of the children's program, it is beneficial to have children commit to attending all three nights. We suggest a Mission title that allows for a number of different sub-themes, depending on parish interests/needs.

With a title such as "A Match Made in Heaven – Learning to Love God More Fully," sub-themes you might consider for the mission sessions could include the following:

1. God knows us
2. God loves us
3. God has given us the gift of ourselves and all creation
4. God speaks to us, and
5. God offers healing, which is not always cure.

When offering a mission for all ages, we believe it is helpful to have two consistent presenters: one to work with the adults and one to work with the children, both giving leadership in the combined group at some time.

What they said

"This mission was terrific. Having it be 'all ages' was what brought me here. My son was excited to come each night and this is what motivated me. In the beginning I came for him. In the end I got more than I expected."

"I've been to hundreds of parish missions and couldn't imagine getting anything out of it with children present. But Nancy challenged me to come the first night and I stayed for all three. I hardly noticed the children leaving and entering the group. The music and content were very good."

"What a great mission! The variety (music) was great, as it gave us a break from listening to a talk all night."

Boy aged 11: "I liked the singing and the snack, but I really like when we leave the church with songs in our heads."

CHAPTER 19

IS LENT FOR KIDS?

Here's a conversation that could easily take place or be overheard in any church during Lent:

"So what have you given up for Lent?"

"I'm letting go of second helpings of dessert. What about you?"

"Chocolate."

"Chocolate! You gotta be kidding! I could never give up chocolate!"

Hearing this, what might children imagine Lent is all about?

Traditionally, Lent – the six weeks leading up to Easter – is a time during which many people believe Christians are called to give alms (food or money given to the poor) and fast, or to perform other acts of purification. People are encouraged to enter a process of self-reflection to see where they are – and are not – living in right relationship with self, others, and God. Many Christians make a sacrifice or give something up for Lent. However it may sound, this is not done to appease God or even to make God love us more fully, for God could not love each of us any more than we are already loved.

Consider that the root of the word "sacrifice" is "to make sacred." A true sacrifice is not meant to diminish or restrict the self. A true sacrifice is meant to lead to more freedom, more love, more peace, more justice. So we fast during Lent in order to feast! We may fast from attachment to what others think of us, and feast on cherishing our own gifts. We may fast from hatred and feast on forgiveness; fast from overwork and feast on quiet time.

How do we decide on the sacrifice – or self-renovation – to undertake during Lent?

Have you ever renovated a house all by yourself? Did you finish on time and within budget? If so, wow! Many people find it difficult and frustrating to do it all themselves; they need a general contractor. But watch out: choose your helper carefully. Some general contractors do shoddy work or ding you for unneeded repairs.

When it comes to our personal renovation, we

have the best possible "general contractor." When his friends and followers were concerned that he would not be with them anymore, Jesus told them that he was sending the Holy Spirit to be their advocate, supporter, and guide. God's Spirit, operating as "General Contractor," will guide us to the sacrifice that is right for each of us. Whatever we are called to "give up" will be something that has restricted our personal "renovation."

This renovation is offered by the Holy Spirit to both children and adults.

HELPING CHILDREN

1. Ask God to guide you to the sacrifice that is right for you. Be receptive to the divine nudge that will focus your Lenten journey. Let the children in your life know how you experienced God's guidance and how you are partnering with God on this. "Today, when I became impatient in the bank lineup, it felt like God was saying in my heart, 'breathe deeply.' So, I did. I calmed down and had a great conversation with the woman behind me."

2. Remember, children already have a relationship with God and already receive divine guidance. They are already in a process of personal renovation. So young children may not need to specify a Lenten sacrifice.

3. If children seem interested in the process of asking God for guidance around personal growth, encourage them to express their desire in prayer. For example, you might say something like, "Abby, once you have asked God for guidance, you may receive a message right away or sometime later. The message may come as a feeling of rightness or peace, or an inner voice, or through another person, or a dream, or in church. So keep your eyes and ears open."

As you and your children journey through Lent, may you know God's support and guidance. When Easter morning dawns and we rejoice at the resurrection of Jesus, we can also rejoice in the resurrected and renovated spirit within us.

Song and Resource References

"Jesus, I'll Stay Awake," Linnea Good, from her CD *Swimmin'
Like a Bird.*

CHAPTER 20

WHY DID JESUS KILL GRANDMA?

Four-year-old Clare told everyone who would listen that it was All Saints' Day. "My saint, St. Clare, has this special day and another special day in the summer," she announced.

Clare's dad and mom went on to tell her that the next day would be All Souls' Day – for all those who had died. Her mother said, "We thought she would be even happier, because my mom had died a few months earlier. To our shock, Clare burst into tears."

"Why did Jesus kill Grandma?" she wailed.

Talking with children about death may feel like one of the hardest challenges adults can face. It takes courage to face our own fears of dying – all the more when it involves our children.

Why would Clare think Jesus killed Grandma?
"But why didn't Jesus make her heart strong? You said to pray for Grandma when she went into the hospital and I did! Why didn't Jesus listen?" Clare pleaded.

At age four, Clare still views her parents as all-powerful – and Jesus as an even more powerful adult. When we say to children that they should pray for healing, it is easy for them to imagine Jesus as holding all the keys to healing and saying "yes" to those he chooses. And so, if we pray and the prayer does not result in what we asked for, it can call into question whether Jesus is fair, whether God is really listening, or whether God really cares.

God's power is love

God's power is not the kind that directly intervenes and manipulates life. God acts as Partner with creation and brings about healing in the midst of the obstacles and circumstances of our lives. Prayer is not a way of convincing God to help us, but rather a way that we can connect to the healing power of God and further direct its path toward others. God offers us love and comfort when we are sad. Children can be encouraged to pray for Grandma, to help spread God's love and healing to her.

It is also important to remember that there is a difference between healing and cure. Sometimes cure does come to us, but all of the time God offers us healing – the strength, love, comfort, and guidance we need to deal with what happens on our life journey.

God's intention is for life

Sometimes we try to make sense of the arbitrariness of a death by saying that God meant for it to happen. We say things like, "God wanted another angel in heaven," or "She was too good for this earth." In this way, we try to imagine a greater purpose to the senseless loss.

God does not kill, nor choose one person over another. Would a loving God take a mother away from her children – even if for a good job in heaven? And by telling children that God needed another angel in heaven, do we subtly warn children *not* to be good or "bait" God? One young boy punched his sister and called out, "See, God, I'm not good! Don't take me to heaven yet!"

Bad things happen. God is present through all of it, guiding and supporting us.

Grieving is good

Many of us worry that if we grieve it shows we don't have faith. We fear that if children see us grieving they will lose faith in us and in God. And yet Jesus grieved a number of times, showing that grief is a healthy response to loss and disappointment. He cried, he groaned, his spirit was heavy. Many psalms describe deep grief and longing for healing.

Grieving is a God-given healing process. In fact, as we grow on our spiritual path, we will actually grieve more frequently, because what touches God's infinite heart will also touch ours. The grief may become more frequent and deep, but it will have a more true and alive quality to it.

Letting our children see our grief can be very helpful. They need to see that there are many different ways to respond to loss. They need to see that our actions and our words say the same thing. If children become upset when they see us cry, it may be because they think we are physically hurt. They may also think it is up to them to make us stop. It can both comfort and clarify for a child to say, "I'm crying because I'm sad about Lisa. When I cry, the pain inside me comes out and I feel better. When *you* feel sad, you hug your teddy and you feel better. Crying helps me feel better."

The facts about death

On the way home from the funeral, Trevor said, "It's snowing and Uncle Tim was only dressed in a suit. Won't he get cold?" Trevor's mom wondered how to explain about dead bodies without giving him nightmares.

Nancy says, "I often gently pull a young child's hair."

"Can you feel that?" she asks.

When the child responds "yes," Nancy cuts off a strand and pulls on it.

"Can you feel it now?" she asks the child again.

"Nope."

Nancy continues: "I then burn the end of that piece of hair, place it in a small hole in the ground, cover it, and invite the child to jump on it.

"Did that make your head hurt?"

"Nope."

"That's because the hair we cut off is no longer attached to the part of you that feels. When someone dies, the part that feels goes to God and what's left is just like that piece of hair. The person isn't in it anymore."

As Nancy explains more fully in her book *A Path Through Loss*, children understand death and have different issues at each stage of their development. Discussions about loss are most helpful when they are appropriate to the child's age. For example, when a young child asks "What happens to us when we die?" we might respond as Linnea once did: "We really don't know. I do believe that, in some way, we go to be in the deep love of God."

Grieving during the Christmas season

Family members may find that grief becomes stronger during Advent and Christmas. They often feel out of step with the world, since everything around them proclaims a time of joy, family togetherness, and eager anticipation.

If it feels overwhelming to try to follow the family practices of past years – tree, lights, etc. – choose a "theme" for the season, such as peace or love. Decorate and pick family activities based on this theme.

Some organizations, such as Hospice, hold a service of prayer and remembrance during Advent, or a special "Blue Christmas" service.

It's all right for adults to feel awkward when children ask questions or make statements about the uncomfortable topics of loss and grief. By being willing to talk about it, and by doing so with love and compassion, we demonstrate, in a small way, the love and compassion in which God holds each of us when we grieve.

Song and Resource References

"Living in the Light," Linnea Good, from her CD *Greatest of These.*

CHAPTER 21

ENDING WELL

Jesus said to her, "Mary!" She turned and said to him in
Hebrew, "Rabbouni!" (which means Teacher).
Jesus said to her, "Do not hold on to me, because
I have not yet ascended to the Father."

John 20:16–17

A few weeks ago, a young mother complained to Nancy, "My three-year-old holds on to my legs and howls like a wild thing when we get to preschool. She doesn't want to leave me. The teacher picks her up and I walk out to the sound of her sobbing. About two minutes later, I peek back into the room to see her happily playing with the other children."

Endings, changes, and transitions! These are difficult for children and adults alike. Like Mary of Magdala, who wanted the old Jesus back, we want things to stay the same.

Endings can be very hard and we don't always do them well. We often prefer to avoid the pain – or to protect each other from it. Trying to hold on to the old, we don't have as much attention and energy for entering the new. Yet an ending done well can be an opportunity for psychological and spiritual growth.

When we take the time to reflect on past relationships, places, and activities, we can cherish them and better understand what they mean to us. We can learn from the past and decide what we want to bring into the future.

The following "Styles for Ending Relationships" list was developed by Nancy for the courses she teaches for lay and professional helpers wanting to minister to grieving and dying adults and children.

Imagine yourself as a youth leader moving to another town, leaving behind a child named Mary.

Unhelpful: Leaving Covertly

You begin to have less frequent or shorter contact with the child or you begin to withdraw emotionally, showing less enthusiasm in your activities with the child, hoping that she will attach to another adult and not feel the loss.

The actual effect on Mary would be more likely that of rejection or abandonment. She may worry that you don't like her anymore. This can negatively affect her self-esteem. She may become angry – and feel guilty about her anger – because the withdrawal is not acknowledged.

Helpful: Leaving Overtly

State your situation and negotiate how to end. "Mary, I will be moving to Ottawa in two months. We can talk about how often we will get together before I go."

With this style of ending, Mary understands the situation, is able to express and deal with the feelings she has about it, and have some power in the manner of ending. Creating a card or some other concrete token of appreciation can help children manage such a transition. This style of ending gives time for this activity.

Unhelpful: Placing Responsibility for Leaving on a Third Party

"I don't want to leave, but my wife/husband says I have to," or, "It's God's will."

Mary is left feeling angry at the other person or at God, and feeling powerless, with unfinished issues.

Helpful: Taking Responsibility

"Mary, I have been talking with my wife/husband about moving for a while and two months from now seems like the best time to go."

Mary can now direct her hurt and angry feelings towards you, and you can help her with them. "I want you to know that I like you very much and my leaving has nothing to do with you." When her feelings are acknowledged and understood, the child finds that her anger moves off quickly and she will not be left with a negative feeling about the "church."

Unhelpful: Leaving without Warning

"This will be the last time we meet."

The reason people often use this style is that they think "a clean, fast break is easier to heal." This is not at all the case. Once hearing this, Mary might go into emotional shock for the remainder of the meeting, giving the impression that she is okay with it.

This style does not give Mary any time to bring up any feelings or concerns with you.

Helpful: Talk about the Ending

Talk about the ending as soon as possible after you have processed your own feelings and issues about it.

Mary is then able to become aware of, and deal with, her reactions over time.

Unhelpful: Keeping It Objective

"Well, that's life. Change happens. " Or, "As Christians, we need to accept change gracefully."

This "philosophy" discourages Mary from expressing her feelings and concerns. She may believe she is a "bad" Christian.

Helpful: Willingness to Self-Disclose

Share the impact the ending has on you. "I'm feeling sad, too, about not seeing you anymore."

Unhelpful: Messy Ending

"It's not really goodbye; I will probably be coming back to visit a few times a year."

This style is such a common one. Users believe it softens the blow. Early in her counselling practice, Nancy used this style of ending. She found that, even years later, when she met a former client at a party or in the grocery store, that person treated her as if the counsellor/client relationship were still active. Once she began to bring closure to the old relationship, she discovered that the two could meet later on a new, and equal, level.

Helpful: Clean Ending

Say a direct goodbye so the other will not misinterpret. "Mary, this is the end of my being your youth worker and your being part of my youth group." This statement gives both a chance to talk about what this relationship has meant to them.

HELPING CHILDREN

1. After reading about the various styles of ending relationships, above, decide which unhelpful endings you practice. We believe everyone practices unhelpful endings at some time. As with so many issues, the most important help we can give

children is to be a role model for healthy spiritual and psychological behaviour. Talk about your endings: "This was Joanna's last day at work, so I told her some of the things I enjoyed about working with her, as I said my goodbyes."

2. Let children grieve the change. Rather than say, "We'll see Grandma at Christmas, so you don't need to cry now," say something like, "I know you love Grandma very much and had a great visit. It's sad to leave."

We frequently hear about the importance of first impressions. We also believe in the importance of last impressions. A healthy style of ending is more likely to result in warm and happy memories of the human interaction, once the goodbyes have been said.

Song and Resource References
"When You Walk from Here," Linnea Good, from her CD *Greatest of These.*

ABOUT THE AUTHORS

Dr. Nancy Reeves is a psychologist, psychotherapist, spiritual director, best-selling author, award-winning columnist, and published poet. She is director and psychotherapist in the Island Loss Clinic, adjunct faculty at the University of Victoria, and has conducted numerous lectures and workshops in nine countries. Nancy has published over 60 articles in professional journals and general interest magazines. She is the recipient of the Victoria YM/YWCA Woman of Distinction Award for her work with children and adults.

Linnea Good is a singer-songwriter helping individuals and churches express their souls through music. She is a leader in the fields of music in worship, biblical storytelling, and all-ages worship. Her background includes a Master of Religious Education degree with a specialty in music as an educational tool; tours to Europe, Australia, New Zealand, and India. The latest of her family CDs, *Swimmin' Like a Bird*, was thrice nominated for major Canadian awards as "Outstanding Children's Album of the Year." She and drummer-spouse, David Jonsson, are based in Summerland, British Columbia, where they co-parent, lead in local choirs, schools, churches and musical events, balancing an extensive touring schedule. You can find her online at www.LinneaGood.com.